ACROSS
BIRMINGHAM
ON THE 29A

DAVID HARVEY

AMBERLEY

Front Cover Photographs

Top

421, (OG 421), stands at the first bus stop in Warren Farm Road having just turned off Kingstanding Road. It is working on the 33 route on 31 July 1943. This AEC Regent 661 had a Vulcan H27/21R body which had been painted grey in 1942. 421 was converted to run on producer gas from 8 June 1943 until it was taken out of service on 30 June 1944 without ever being repainted in fleet livery on this date. It is waiting with its anthracite-burning trailer for another painfully slow journey to the Finchley Road terminus. In 1942 the Ministry of War Transport issued instructions that 10 per cent of motorbus fleets with a strength of more than 100 vehicles had to be converted to producer-gas operation, and 421 was one of twenty-five petrol-engined Regents to be converted. That the long 33 route was the only route chosen to use this system was surprising, as this route had several long, steep hills causing the buses to cough and smoke their way slowly up Kingstanding Road's long climbs. (L. W. Perkins)

Bottom

In miserable weather on 24 November 2012, 4673 (BX 54 XRL), a Volvo B7TL with a Wright H43/29F body, turns into Baldwins Lane when working on a city-bound 5 service from Solihull. This National Express West Midlands double-decker is passing the Baldwin public house, the long-time location of the former BCT 29A route. (D. R. Harvey)

Rear Cover Photograph

The driver and conductor stand by the Bundy Clock at the terminus of the 29 route in Highfield Road. Their bus, 2860 (JOJ 860), a Daimler CVG6 with a Crossley H30/25R body, had entered service on 1 February 1953 and was one of the last of the class of 125 buses to have the seating capacity written across the lower back panel. 2860 is still fitted with the decorative hub caps, which were usually derogatorily referred to as 'dustbin lids'. The bus is standing in Highfield Road at the terminus of the 29 route in around 1954 and is carrying an advertisement for the long-forgotten De Reszke full-strength cigarettes. (D. Griffiths)

First published 2013

Amberley Publishing
The Hill, Stroud
Gloucestershire, GL5 4EP

www.amberley-books.com

British Library Cataloguing in Publication Data.
A catalogue record for this book is available from the British Library.

ISBN 978 1 4456 1621 6
e-book ISBN 978 1 4456 1636 0

Typeset in 10pt on 12pt Sabon.
Typesetting and Origination by Amberley Publishing.
Printed in the UK.

Introduction

This is a journey across the City of Birmingham, geographically following the 29A service and the various associated bus routes instigated by the Corporation by the ever more complex route developments. It also shows the changes through time in the city from the late 1920s until the present day.

The story begins in the north of Birmingham, in the second-largest municipal housing estate in 1920s Europe, through the industrial areas of Hockley, the Jewellery Quarter, Newtown and into the then still largely Victorian city centre. The various routes taken by all the bus services, operated successively by Birmingham City Transport until 1969, West Midlands Travel until 1986, Travel West Midlands and latterly National Express West Midlands, show buses in an ever-changing and thriving central area. The effects of the wartime bombing in Birmingham and the brutal redevelopments associated with the 1960s all reveal a change from the early supremacy of the pedestrian to the period when the city was dominated by the needs of the car, and pedestrians were reduced to a troglodyte existence in dingy underpasses.

If by the twenty-first century Birmingham has reached the sunny highlands of a new era of urban planning, then that can only be a good thing, but social changes have altered the urban make-up and some suburbs, which were at one time thriving communities, have for ever changed in the new multicultural Birmingham.

The buses have developed from open rear-staircase vehicles with open driver's cabs throughout the period between 1934 and 1954, when the Birmingham Standard bus developed into the epitome of urban comfort, with wood- and leather-lined saloons with deeply upholstered seats downstairs and a gentlemen's smoking room on top. Economics and one-man-operation led to the rear-engined, front-entrance double-decker becoming, in ever more advanced forms, the standard double-decker, though after deregulation the use of single-deck vehicles became more common.

The 29A bus route was the longest variation of the routes that ran across the city from outside the city boundary in the north at the Pheasey Estate in Aldridge via Birmingham's city centre to Baldwin's Lane, Hall Green, in the south, literally yards from the Solihull boundary. At its greatest length this route was around 23 miles long, making it the second-longest bus service after the famous Outer Circle 11 route.

The original service was the 29, introduced on 6 February 1928 between The Boar's Head public house on Aldridge Road, Perry Barr, and Highfield Road, Hall Green, across the city near to Yardley Wood railway station in an area of privately owned semi-detached housing, characterised by half-round bay windows. On 26 August 1929 the 29 was diverted from Six Ways, Aston and Summer Lane to go via Hockley Brook into the city through the heavily industrialised area between the huge Joseph Lucas factory and the famous Jewellery Quarter. When the 33 route was begun it went into the city by way of the original 29 route. This was quickly extended on 5 November 1930 to Ellerton Road via Kingstanding Road and Warren Farm Road to serve the rapidly expanding municipal housing estate being constructed in Kingstanding. The ever-increasing traffic demands as the huge housing estate grew involved the addition of a second bus service, the 33 route, which also terminated initially at Ellerton Road and was introduced on 18 August 1930. This was extended to Finchley Road at the junction with Kings Road on 2 January 1933. Another cross-city bus service was introduced on 12 January 1931 when the 34 bus from Hagley Road, which had only replaced the unwanted and unpopular tram service to the Kings Head pub six months earlier, was linked to the 33 route via a labyrinthine route through the back streets of the city centre. Another cross-city service to be introduced was the 25 route, which started at Finchley Road – as did the 33 and 34 – but then followed the 29 though Lozells and Hockley to Hall Green.

Between 1933 and 1936 Birmingham City Council introduced variations on their famous (or infamous if one was a visitor) One-Way Street Scheme around the city centre, which affected all the cross-city services as well as those terminating somewhere within the city-centre loop of High Street, New Street, Corporation Street, Bull Street and Colmore Row. It was during this time that the 29A route began operation, using the same route as the 29 from Kingstanding Circle until it reached Stratford Road, Springfield, whereupon it diverted through the edge of Moseley by way of tree-lined dual carriageways and more 1930s owner-occupied semi-detached housing before reaching the suburban terminus at Baldwin's Lane, another part of Hall Green and only around half a mile from the original 29 route terminus. The wartime period from 1939 until 1945 inevitably saw cutbacks in the frequency of bus services and various shortenings of outer termini during the late evening, while both the 25 and 34 routes became 'peak hours only' with the former route ceasing to be cross-city. The main exception to this was the extension of the 29A route on 21 April 1941 across the city boundary into the Pheasey Estate at Collingwood Drive.

After the end of the Second World War most of Birmingham's bus routes returned to their pre-war situation, although a night service, serving the Kingstanding area and numbered NS29A, was introduced on 25 August 1947, and on New Year's Day 1950 the 33 service was diverted from Alma Street and Summer Lane into Newtown Row to replace the abandoned 6 tram route. The terminus of the 33 route was moved out of Martineau Street into Union Street on 16 October 1960; Union Street in turn was closed to traffic when it was pedestrianised in the mid-1980s and the 33 route then terminated in Dale End. Meanwhile, the biggest change was the renumbering of the 29 and 29A routes on 29 November 1964, with the former becoming the 29 for southward journeys and 30 for northbound journeys. The 29A route became the 90 for northbound journeys and 91 for southbound journeys.

With the exception of the introduction of the 98 express bus service from New Street to Kingstanding Circle via Snow Hill, Summer Lane, Six Ways, Aston and Perry Barr underpass, the bus services remained stable until the end of Corporation operation on

1 October 1969, when West Midlands PTE took over all the bus services. The southern sections of the former 29 and 29A routes gradually became more of a problem, and a lot of dead mileage to and from Yardley Wood garage was the prime reason for the subsequent alterations. These occurred on 28 February 1971 when the 90 was altered to run from Baldwins Lane to the city, the 91 southbound to Baldwins Lane and the new 92 service replaced the former 37 route to the Hall Green boundary. The 92 was later extended through Shirley to Monkspath. The 25 route was abandoned as a peak-hour service at this time, and the cross-city 34 route also suffered the same fate a few years later.

Throughout the rest of the 1970s and until deregulation, there were numerous comparatively minor route adjustments but after deregulation on 26 October 1986, West Midlands Travel abandoned any cross-city connection, leaving the 33 to be extended from Finchley Road via Kings Road to Pheasey Estate. In April 1995, the company was purchased by the National Express Group and rebranded as Travel West Midlands in September 1996. One of their first major upgrading initiatives took place on 16 February 1997, when the 33 service was designated Line 33 and had route-dedicated buses allocated to the service. The two southern routes – the 91 via Baldwins Lane and the 92 directly along Stratford Road via Sparkbrook, Sparkhill and Hall Green – were renumbered 5 and 6 respectively and both were extended to Solihull station via Shirley. 5 travels beyond the old 92 terminus at Cranmore Boulevard by way of Monkspath and Widney Manor station, while the 6 reaches its terminus via Blossomfield Road. This is the situation today, although since 4 February 2008 the fleet name has been National Express West Midlands.

Acknowledgements

The author is grateful to the many photographers acknowledged in the text who have contributed to this volume. I sincerely thank all of those who are still alive for allowing me to use pictures, many of which were taken more than sixty years ago. Where the photographer is not known, the photographs are credited to my own collection.

Special thanks are due to my wife Diana for her splendid proofreading and allowing me the time to research and write this book. Roger Smith's excellent maps are wonderfully informative and help the reader to place the photographs in their correct location. The book would not have been possible without the continued encouragement given by Louis Archard and Campbell McCutcheon of Amberley Publishing.

Route Maps

The northern routes: the bus services from Pheasey Estate and Kingstanding on the 25, 29, 29A, 30, 33, 34, 90 and 91 to the city centre.

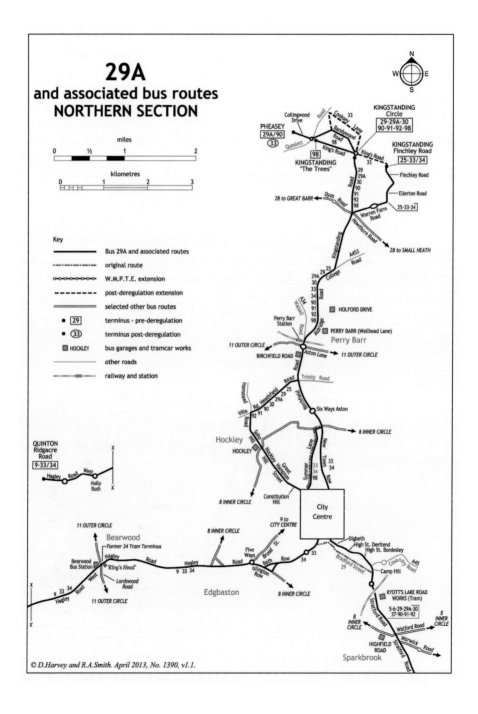

The southern routes: the bus services from the city centre to Sparkbrook, Sparkhill, Yardley Wood, Hall Green, Shirley and Solihull on the 29, 29A, 30, 90, 91, 92, 5 and 6 routes.

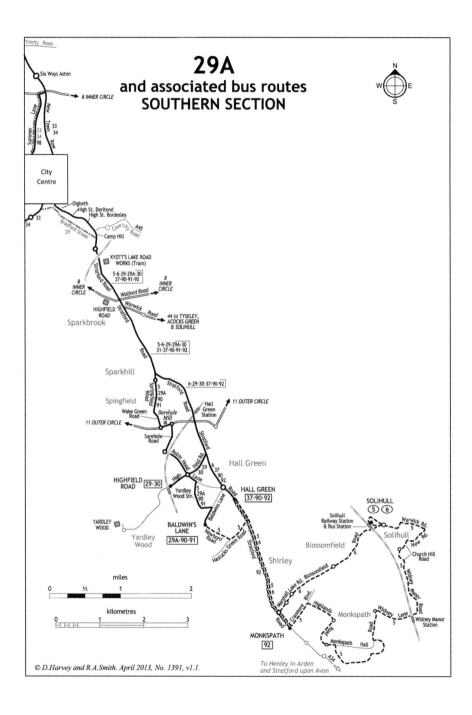

© D.Harvey and R.A.Smith. April 2013, No. 1391, v1.1.

The Northern Half

Pheasey–Hawthorn Road
29A, 90 and 33 Routes

The Pheasey Estate to Hawthorn Road section of these bus routes began at one of the highest parts of the West Midlands and was also outside the City in Aldridge. The terminus was in Collingwood Drive at around 530 feet in Aldridge in a post-war council-owned housing estate. The route descended a steep hill before crossing Queslett Road and over the boundary into Birmingham. This part of Kingstanding centred on Bandywood Road was, like the housing in Aldridge, was developed in the 1950s. The route arrived at Kingstanding Circle which although not at the geographical heart of the huge 1920s Kingstanding municipal housing estate, was the shopping centre for the area. The section of the route from the Birmingham boundary at Queslett Road had been very poor quality farmland on this fairly bleak upland area where farmers had for years struggled to get a good living. Birmingham Council's plan to develop one of the largest municipal housing estates in Europe at that time was a huge financial opportunity for the farmers and they grabbed the chance to take the money and sell up. Very soon the newly laid out suburb contained a variety of well-built comfortable housing and was quickly occupied by families coming out of the Inner City slums. On leaving the Circle, the bus services entered Kingstanding Road, which although lined with more interwar council houses, was a much older highway, specifically being part of the Roman Ryknield Street. Many of the side roads were named after suburban areas in London because one of the main building contractors was based in the Capital. The road had wide grass verges on the western side and was designed to carry the tram tracks which were never built. The first shopping area after the Circle was in Hawthorn Road and spilled across the junction with Kingstanding Road and Warren Farm Road.

Opposite above: Before the shops were built at the traffic island in Collingwood Drive where Hillingford Avenue crossed, exposed-radiator Crossley DD42/6, 2360 (JOJ 360), stands at the terminus of the 29A route in around 1957 with the Pheasey Library building behind the distant pillar box. During the Second World War, the library building had been requisitioned by the military and the remnants of the old wooden army barracks stand beyond the road sign. Alongside the bus is an old caravan, which is being used as a rest room by the drivers. Although something of a rarity, until housing and shops were constructed, caravans were used for this purpose elsewhere in the city, notably at the 94 trolleybus terminus at the Coventry Road city boundary, at Arden Oak Road and at the terminus of the 14 bus route at Kitts Green. (D. R. Harvey Collection)

The 29A route was the northern extension of the 29 route from Kingstanding Circle by way of Lambeth Road and across the Birmingham boundary, terminating at Collingwood Drive. This required an agreement with Midland Red and the new service was implemented on 21 April 1941. To celebrate its then twenty years in preservation, the author undertook to take his former Birmingham Crossley 2489 (JOJ 489) on a tour of all the Corporation bus routes that the bus could have operated in its working life between July 1950 and its withdrawal in March 1969. This tour took place on Sunday 2 April 1989 (2489, get it?), on an appallingly wet and gloomy day. 2489 is a Crossley DD42/6 with a Crossley H30/24R body and stands at the city-bound bus stop of the former 29A route in Collingwood Drive. Further photographs of this tour will appear elsewhere in the appropriate locations. (D. R. Harvey)

The driver and conductor of 2094 (JOJ 94) stand near to the Bundy Clock at the terminus of the 29A route in Collingwood Drive in around 1961 with the shops on the corner of Hillingford Avenue behind. This Daimler CVD6 was one of Yardley Wood garage's allocation of around twenty-seven and it entered service on 1 March 1951. The 100 'New Look' concealed-radiator Daimler CVD6s were ordered with Metro-Cammell bodies in 1949 but their construction was badly delayed at the bodybuilders. They were delightfully quiet and sophisticated buses, but their Daimler CD6 engines tended to burn engine oil and maintenance costs were higher than contemporary buses. As a result they had somewhat short lives with 2094 being withdrawn at the end of July 1965. (A. D. Broughall)

Opposite above: Looking back along Collingwood Drive, towards Queslett Road and the Birmingham city boundary at the Pheasey Estate terminus of the 29A route, is 1717 (HOV 716). By around 1962, this Brush-bodied Leyland Titan PD2 Sp was one of the fifty-seven allocated to Perry Barr garage. 1716 had entered service on 1 January 1949 and spent its entire nineteen-year BCT career on that garage's arduous routes. On the opposite side of the road is a 1955 Morris Minor, which is the only other vehicle in Collingwood Drive. Although housing development began in the 1930s, in the Second World War some completed houses were requisitioned by the War Office for use by American troops, who stayed there until after the war. The Pheasey Estate consisted of both private and council houses, which were built in completely different styles, though the earlier houses were very similar in construction to those in adjacent areas of Birmingham. (A. D. Broughall)

Opposite below: West Midlands PTE initially ordered seventy-five Leyland Titan TNLXBs with Park Royal H47/26Fs, but industrial problems at Park Royal meant that most of the order was cancelled. Only five were delivered and these were numbered 7001 to 7005. On 6 July 1979, 7004 (WDA 4T), initially the one Titan to be allocated to Perry Barr garage, stands at the outbound terminus of the 90 route in Collingwood Drive alongside the short section of dual carriageway. The Five West Midlands Titans were taken out of service and sold in 1983 to the London Transport Executive as their T1126–1130 as training buses but within a short time were converted to operate with coach seats. (D. R. Harvey Collection)

On 9 July 2003, 4475 (BJ 03 EWF), a Volvo B7TL with a Wright seventy-two-seater body, stands in the same spot outside Pheasey Library and the associated Collingwood Centre as 7004. This was the first bus in a batch of fifty vehicles and was just over one month old when it arrived via the original Finchley Road terminus by way of Kings Road and Kingstanding Circle when working on the 33 route. The 90 service was renumbered 33 on 26 October 1986. On 16 February 1997 the Line 33 route was introduced as the first Showcase route in the city, with route-dedicated buses and bus stops giving electronic timetable details. Some fourteen of these new buses were allocated to Perry Barr garage to work on the Line 33 route. (D. R. Harvey)

The terminus of the 29A route in Collingwood Drive was along a long flat section of road lined by early post-war semi-detached houses. From Queslett Road, the terminus was reached by a steep climb and Park Royal-bodied Daimler 'Fleetline' CRG6LX 4092, (YOX 92K), has just descended the hill when working on the 90 route. These buses were among the first to be ordered by the newly formed West Midlands PTE and this one entered service in September 1971. It is turning into the lay-by in front of the Trees public house on Queslett Road. This unusual road name is derived from the Old English word 'queese', which was a wood pigeon, and 'slaed', referring to a valley. (L. Mason)

Travelling towards Birmingham on 30 March 2004 is 4478, (BJ03 EWK). This Wright-bodied Volvo B7TL was route-branded 33 LINE, having replaced five-year-old Volvo B10L single-deckers on the route. This part of Kingstanding between The Circle and Queslett Road was developed in the early post-war years and roads such as Kettlehouse Road, Bandywood Road and Lambeth Road were lined with blocks of low-rise housing. This area was previously prime farmland with large farms at Kettlehouse and Warren. (D. R. Harvey)

The centre of the huge 1920s municipal housing estate was The Circle, built on the site of Icknield or Ryknield Street, a Roman road linking the Fosse Way – near Bourton-on-the-Water by way of Bidford, Alcester and across Birmingham from Kings Norton, Stirchley – to the Roman camp at Metchley, established around 48 AD as a base camp for the conquest of the Birmingham area. Although largely lost in the present-day city centre, though the name is found today in Icknield Street near the Jewellery Quarter, the road reappears at Perry Bridge over the River Tame and then follows the line of Kingstanding Road, until it enters Sutton Park where a preserved section of the Roman road can be seen. It then follows the line of the present-day A38 from Lichfield to Derby. With Kings Road running from top to bottom and Kingstanding Road leading towards the city centre on the right, the wide open spaces of the geometrically laid-out Kingstanding Circle are revealed in this 1936 view. A bus working on the 29 route stands in front of the set-back row of shops and just in front of the impressive wooden bus shelter. The double-decker is a still fairly new Morris-Commercial Imperial with a Metro-Cammell fifty-seater dating from 1933. These buses were numbered 507 to 553 and were purchased in order to support local industry. Of the eighty-three Imperials constructed, Birmingham operated fifty-one. Unfortunately, while the all-metal-framed bodywork was excellent, the Morris chassis and engine were somewhat frail and withdrawals began as early as 1939. In the foreground is a Belisha Beacon named after Leslie Hore-Belisha, the Minister of Transport, which was introduced in the UK as a road safety feature in 1935, but without the black and white zebra crossing markings, which were only introduced in 1951. (D. R. Harvey)

The 29 cross-city route to Hall Green had shortworkings into Birmingham which somewhat unhelpfully carried the destination display of CITY. One of Birchfield Road garage's Daimler COG5s, 953, (COX 953), waits at the Bundy Clock on Kingstanding Circle in front of George Mason's grocery and provision store in the early 1950s. The bus driver takes on the almost obligatory stance of resigned boredom as he waits for his departure time to slowly come round. After a period in store, 953 was resurrected in May 1958 and spent two years working from Acocks Green garage until it was withdrawn on New Year's Eve 1959. (D. R. Harvey)

One of the 'unfrozen' Leyland Titan TD7s with a Leyland H30/26R body originally intended for Western SMT waits outside the Kingstanding Circle branch of Wilkins chemist's. The bus, which arrived in Birmingham in 1942, is about to work back to Highfield Road on the 29 service. The driver is about to get into the cab and is still smiling despite having to manage a gearbox which had a very slow gear change. Despite being built from parts already in stock at Leyland Motors when the Government allowed buses to be built again, 1325 was built to a pre-war finish and survived in service until the autumn of 1954. (D. Barlow)

Viewed from in front of the row of 1930s shops on The Circle across the wide expanse of grass on the traffic island, towering over the area is the Kingstanding Odeon. This was designed by Harry Weedon, and with its Art Deco styling was the first of Oscar Deutsch's cinemas to be built in this distinctive style. The Odeon opened on 22 July 1935 with the showing of *The Lives of a Bengal Lancer* starring Gary Cooper and it remained a popular venue until it closed in December 1962. To the left of the pair of Corporation buses is the impressive brick and wrought-iron archway to the Kingstanding Public House. This large 'roadhouse' public house had been opened in early October 1933 but was closed in 1965; subsequently, there have been two further licensed premises on the site. The bus on the left is 2001, a Daimler CVD6 with a Metro-Cammell H30/24R body and the proud carrier of the registration JOJ 1, which today would be much prized. This is working on the 29 route, which terminated at The Circle. It is being passed by 2381 (JOJ 381), a Crossley DD42/6 with a Crossley body, which is about to turn up Kettlehouse Road and on to the Pheasey Estate terminus of the 29A route. Both buses date from 1950 and both are carrying large rear fleet numbers, which were discontinued in 1953. (Commercial postcard)

Opposite above: The first buses ordered by West Midlands PTE were a batch of 100 Daimler Fleetline CRG6LXs with Park Royal H43/33F bodies, whose style had origins in the ill-fated 33-foot-long 'Jumbos' ordered by BCT in 1969. 4094, (YOX 84K), was one of the last buses delivered from Park Royal with the BCT-style khaki roof, entering service in September 1971. This bus was allocated to Hockley garage, which still had turns on the Kingstanding service. 4094 has turned into Kingstanding Road on the 92 service to Hall Green and is passing an Austin Cambridge A60 with a Farina-designed body parked on the somewhat worn grass verge. (D. R. Harvey)

Waiting at the bus stop just beyond Dunedin Road in early 1969 is 3659, (JOL 659E). The bus is working on the limited-stop 98 service, which was introduced on 1 April 1968 and ran from outside the Odeon in New Street by way of Snow Hill, Summer Lane, Alma Street, Six Ways and Perry Barr. The single-decker is one of twelve Ford R192s fitted with Ford 5.42-litre engines mounted in front of the set-back front axle. They had bodies built by Strachan with their 'Pacesaver' body, which had a B46F layout, but constructed to BCT specifications. 3659 had entered service on 1 April 1967, and after being transferred to WMPTE on 1 October 1969 survived in service until 31 August 1977, when they were replaced by new dual-purpose Leyland Nationals. (D. R. Harvey)

Above: After November 1964, the northbound 29A route was renumbered 90 and so it was that one of Perry Barr's Leyland Titan PD2 Sps, built with modifications peculiar to BCT's requirements, travelled northbound along Kingstanding Road some years before this section of the road was converted to dual carriageway. 1704 (HOV 704) is dropping off passengers just beyond the Hare and Hounds public house. The Brush H30/24R metal-framed bodies on Leyland PD2 chassis were unique to Birmingham, though some forty similar bodies, but built without the BCT-style straight staircase, were built on AEC Regent III chassis, the bulk of which went to Leicester City Transport. (W. A. Camwell)

On leaving the Hotspur Road bus stop, the 29/29A inbound service descended towards the five-way junction at Hawthorn Road where it would meet up with the 25 peak-time service and the 33 route coming out of Warren Farm Road, both of which terminated at Finchley Road. On 22 July 1969, 2889 (JOJ 889), one of Yardley Wood garage's Daimler CVG6s with a fifty-five-seat Crossley body, is working on the 29 route back to Highfield Road near to Yardley Wood railway station. 2889 was one of the class that didn't have a particularly long life after being absorbed into the WMPTE fleet in October 1969 as it was withdrawn in early January 1971. Because of poor delivery dates of new buses in the early 1970s and the necessity to withdraw some of the buses inherited from the erstwhile Walsall and Wolverhampton fleets, some of these Daimler CVG6s had to soldier on until October 1977. (A. Yates)

The buses provided by Hockley garage for its share of the 29 group of services were usually Leyland-bodied Leyland Titan PD2/1s, but less frequently one of their Park Royal-bodied buses would be turned out. Here 2181 (JOJ 181), the first bus of the day, has just left the rudimentary utility bus shelter in Kingstanding Road, near to the junction with Dyas Road, as it travels towards the 29 route terminus at Kingstanding Circle, which might have been a more logical destination to display than KINGS ROAD. As a child, your author remembers going into a Bywaters pork butcher's located then in the block of shops behind the Hillman Minx Series III saloon and eating one of their magnificent steak and kidney pies. They were a Birmingham-based pie manufacturer who also specialised in pork products, but by the time 2181 was travelling along Kingstanding Road, they had closed down. Numbered 2181–2230, they were the only PD2/1s ever to receive this style of Park Royal body. The first fifteen buses were delivered with the front destination box set around 3 inches too high. As a result, the middle blue livery band above the cab was straight and did not dip beneath the route display. From bus 2196, the destination box was lowered and the blue livery band had a dip in it and a thinner centre section. This variation in livery roughly marked the division of their allocation, with usually around the first fourteen of the class being garaged at Hockley while the remaining larger group of thirty-six were at Rosebery Street garage. (A. Yates)

Travelling into the city on a 29 service is Metro-Cammell-bodied Daimler CVG6 1563 (GOE 563). This bus had been transferred from Cotteridge garage to Birchfield Road during 1963, remaining there until it was withdrawn in July 1966. With an A. D. Wimbush's bakery, a Maypole grocer's and Marsh's butcher's occupying the prominent corner of Kingstanding Road and Warren Farm Road, the bus will already be braking for the stop just over the brow of the hill at the start of the section of road that had been built a dual carriageway. Crossing Kingstanding Road at this point was the 28A bus service, which came out of Dyas Road on the right, where it terminated at the bottom of a quite fearsomely steep hill. (A. Yates)

33 and 34 Routes Between Finchley Road and Hawthorn Road

This is the real heartland of the huge Kingstanding housing estate and took the 33 bus route from Kings Road at about 460 feet above sea level to Kingstanding Road by way of the hilly terrain in the Warren Farm Road area. Other than churches, schools and a community hall there were few amenities save for the 33 bus route, which traversed what were largely side roads lined with council-built housing.

At deregulation on 26 October 1986, the 90 route was renumbered 33 and this was extended from Finchley Road along Kings Road before rejoining the old 29A/90 route to Collingwood Drive, Pheasey. Having left the former terminus of the original 33 route in Finchley Road, 4479, (BJ03 EWL), works on this linking section and approaches Kingstanding Circle in Kings Road. This Volvo B7TL with a Wright H43/29F body was already five years old when seen on 16 January 2008. (D. R. Harvey)

In the heart of the Kingstanding municipal housing estate is Finchley Road, lined by the typical terraced housing blocks that so characterised this enormous housing estate. Most of the houses were of the three-bedroom, none-parlour type, either built as semi-detached or in terraced blocks of four individual dwellings. The terminus of the original 33 bus route was at the top of Finchley Road, at the junction with Kings Road. This was at a height above sea level of around 520 feet, and even when the council housing was completed, the whole of the Kingstanding area was locally known as 'Little Russia' on account of the cold chill winds that seemed always seemed to be blowing from the east into the bleak area. Although the 33 route was originally introduced as far as Ellerton Road on 5 November 1930, it was not extended to Finchley Road on 2 January 1933. With Kings Road in the background, 3398 (398 KOV), which entered service on 6 November 1964, loads up with passengers prior to heading off to the city. The bus is a Daimler Fleetline CRG6LX with an MCCW H39/33F body and was one of the last ten, numbered 3391–3400, built with redesigned windscreens and front panels. 3398 was one of four of these last ten to have a curved, rather than a V-shaped, windscreen, giving these buses a much more modern appearance than the earlier buses. (D. R. Harvey)

Kingstanding was part of Perry Barr UDC until 1928, and at that time contained just four farms on the exposed heathland that rose steeply to the north of the River Tame. Just as when Quinton was taken over in 1909, Kingstanding was seen as an ideal site to build a new municipal housing estate to take people out of the squalor of the blighted back-to-back housing in the inner-city areas. Birmingham Council was quickly off the mark and by 1932 some 6,302 houses had been built, providing homes for 30,000 people, whose demand for public transport led to the introduction of the 33 bus service. The last tram route extension had been opened to another similar municipal housing estate in Stechford on Tuesday 26 August 1928, so Kingstanding might have been similarly served from the Perry Barr terminus of the 6 tram route. Most of the new main roads, such as Aldridge Road, College Road and Kingstanding Road, were built with either central reservations or extensive areas of grass on one side of the road. The Corporation had the Parliamentary powers to do this, so it was perhaps surprising that for the first time motorbuses were introduced, on 18 August 1930 to Ellerton Road. Standing at the Finchley Road/Kings Road terminus of the 33 route on Saturday 31 July 1943 is 392 (OG 392). This 1930-vintage petrol-engined AEC Regent 661 with an English Electric H27/21R body had been converted to run on the inefficient producer-gas system just one month earlier. This government attempt to conserve precious petrol supplies was not successful despite a huge capital investment at Perry Barr garage, from where all the gas-powered buses operated. (L. W. Perkins)

On the original Kingstanding Estate, there was just one church, one church hall, one new public house and one cinema. It was left to the residents to build their own community centres and set up their own places of entertainment and religious observation. In Warren Farm Road is one such church. This is the large brick-built Christ the King Roman Catholic church, which dates from the early 1950s and contains some fine examples of stained glass from the 1950s and 1960s. The bus working towards Finchley Road on the 33 route is Brush-bodied Leyland Titan PD2 Sp 1733 (HOV 733). These 100 Leylands were modified PD2/1 models with some chassis modifications for BCT. When the author was a very little boy, 1733 was his favourite Birmingham bus. (D. Hill)

The large crescent shape of Warren Farm Road had a one-way system around the large central grass area. Christ the King RC church is behind the bus, which is beginning the steep climb up towards the junction with Hawthorn and Kingstanding Roads. The bus is 3114 (MOF 114), one of twenty-nine Daimler CVG6s with a Crossley H30/25R body, which had entered service from Miller Street garage on 1 July 1953 in time for the final tram closure of the three Erdington routes just four days later. By the early 1960s, 3114 was garaged at Perry Barr but during 1962 it moved to Birchfield Road garage. It is climbing up Warren Farm Road and is about to pass the municipal houses on the corner of Danesbury Crescent near to Cranbourne Road. (D. R. Harvey)

Opposite above: On 28 August 1964, 3072, (MOF 72), followed by a rear-engined Renault Dauphine, has reached the short flat section of Warren Farm Road before it meets the Kingstanding Road junction. Warren Farm was one of four in the area that were demolished in 1928 as part of the Kingstanding municipal housing development. This Guy Arab IV with a Gardner 6LW engine and a Metro-Cammell H30/25R body had entered service on 1 February 1954 and spent most of its Corporation years operating from Quinton garage on the 3A route to Ridgacre Lane, the 9 to the Hagley Road West boundary and occasional forays into north Birmingham on the 34 route. On the left is one of the utility steel pole and corrugated iron structures that were euphemistically called bus 'shelters', although in reality the distant trees offered more protection from the elements. (A. Yates)

Opposite below: In virtually the same position as 421, (OG 421), seen on the front cover, in around 1962 is Crossley-bodied Crossley DD42/6 2362, (JOJ 362), working on the 33 route. It stands at the bus stop in Warren Farm Road outside the baker's shop owned by Small Heath-based A. D. Wimbush. These buses, along with the next batch of thirty Crossleys, were the only exposed-radiator double-deckers to have sliding saloon ventilators. Perry Barr garage's Crossleys had 8.6-litre Crossley HOE7/4B cross-flow engines, but some fifty of them, including 2362, had been converted to the downdraught cylinder heads in around 1954, which improved their all-round performance. Like the Brush-bodied Leylands, the Crossleys had a synchromesh gearbox, which was surprisingly easier to use than those found on the Leylands. Unfortunately, the Crossleys weighed in at 8 tons 7 cwt 1 qtr and were considerably down on power when compared to the Leyland o. 600 9.8-litre Leyland-engined Brush-bodied bus, which weighed in at 8 tons 1 cwt 3 qtrs. Behind the bus is Kingstanding Road, with Dyas Road on the other side of the junction. Parked in front of the Crossley is a 1958 Austin A55 Cambridge. (D. R. Harvey)

Hawthorn Road–Aldridge Road
25, 29, 29A, 30, 33, 34, 90 and 91 Routes

The Kingstanding Road Junction with Hawthorn Road was very exposed as it was some 180 feet above Perry Barr Park at Aldridge Road only about one mile to the south. The straight Kingstanding Road descended to the junction with College Road passing through, for the first time since the outer termini of all the routes, 1930s semi-detached private housing of the sort which was recreated twenty-five years later by Bayco Building Sets which was a children's construction kit using a base with holes in it, steel rods and plastic bricks, windows and roofs based on round-bayed interwar housing designs. Towards the junction of College Road the road was lined with bungalows. From Hawthorn Road to Crossway Lane there was a central reservation which suggested it was designed for tram tracks, but from Crossway Lane to College Road there was a wide expanse of land and a single carriageway which remained for over forty years before Kingstanding Road was completed as a dual carriageway. The city bound buses turned into College Road and almost immediately crossed the Tame Valley Canal which was still in use commercially well into the 1960s. The original 29 bus terminus was at the junction of College Road and Aldridge Road in front of the Boar's Head Public House. THe route passed Perry Barr Park and crossed the River Tame on a 1930s bridge which had succeeded the eighteenth-century Zig-Zag Bridge before heading towards Perry Barr.

Above: Kingstanding overlooked Birmingham on its northern side, and even before the area was acquired for housing, the farms in the area were not generally prosperous, as the soils were poor and the upland area very bleak, having originally being a heathland with a few areas of woodland. Many years later when the estate, then the second-largest municipal housing area in Europe, had been completed, the new residents, many of them coming from areas such as Summer Lane and Alma Street, where conditions in the Victorian back-to-backs were appalling, complained about the constant cold easterly winds which made living conditions very trying. One of the most exposed spots on the 29/29A route was at the junction of Kingstanding Road and Hawthorn Road. Just behind the bus is a large green-painted wooden and glass passenger shelter built for protection from the elements. These shelters were more usually found at tram or bus termini. The bus is 1510 (GOE 510), one of Birchfield Road garage's AEC-engined Daimler CVD6s with a Metro-Cammell body. This bus entered service in 1948 and is working from the Kingstanding Circle on a 29 route shortworking, going only as far as the Co-operative department store in High Street. So as not to confuse intending passengers by showing 29 (which went to Highfield Road, Hall Green), 1510 is showing CITY, meaning that it was on a 29 shortworking, which was probably even more confusing! (A. Yates)

Opposite: Turning across Hawthorn Road into Kingstanding Road is 1552 (GOE 552), a Daimler CVA6 with an H30/24R body, which had entered service on 1 November 1947. The bus is displaying the detailed 25 route destination display, revealing that the route went into the city by way of Heathfield Road. These buses were the only ones built for BCT by Metro-Cammell with a thin pillared-style body that was similar to their pre-war bodies for Birmingham. As a result they weighed only 7 tons 12 cwt, up to 7 cwt lighter than subsequent exposed-radiator buses. Their light weight was just as well as they were fitted with the AEC A173 oil engine of 7.58-litre capacity. 1552 was withdrawn on 31 October 1963, just after the Ford Consul Classic 116E saloon car, behind the bus, had been delivered to its proud owner. (A. Yates)

Above: Speeding down the hill in Kingstanding Road from the distant junction with Hawthorn Road in around 1963 is 1553 (GOE 553). The bus is passing the junction with Melverley Grove as it travels to the city on the 25 route, and is passing the Territorial Army barracks on the other side of the dual carriageway. Lining the road on the right are the privately built houses that dated from the 1930s and were quite distinctive from the houses in the huge municipal estate beyond Hawthorn Road. The bus is a Daimler CVA6 with a Metro-Cammell body and entered service on 1 November 1947. Overtaking the bus is an Austin A40 Somerset saloon. (D. R. Harvey Collection)

Opposite above: Waiting at the impressive bus shelter in Kingstanding Road is 2564 (JOJ 564), one of Quinton garage's many Guy Arab III Specials with the economical and efficient Gardner 6LW 8.4-litre engine. These 26-foot-long buses were splendidly solid and powerful beasts with a lovely rasping exhaust note, though their propensity to suffer from brake fade resulted in nearly all the 'New Look'-front buses having their front wings shortened to improve the airflow onto the front drums. It is working on the cross-city 34 route to Quinton in around 1969. The original Ellerton Road terminus was also the starting point of the southbound Cross City 34 route, which was introduced on 12 January 1931 as a tram replacement service to Five Ways before heading west along Hagley Road towards the Kings Head terminus. Northbound services from Quinton were numbered 33. (A. Yates)

Opposite below: The use of buses on the newly constructed Kingstanding Road was one of the first departures from building a tram route on the main arterial roads of the city. The construction, along parts of the road, of a wide dual carriageway is a reminder that when first planned the road had been designed for trams to run on a central reservation. 1131 (CVP 231), travels up the hill in Kingstanding Road with the Territorial Army barracks to the right of the Ford Anglia 100E saloon. It is working on the 25 route to Finchley Road and has already moved over to the right of the dual carriageway in order to get into position to turn into Warren Farm Road. Entering service on 17 November 1937, this MCCW-bodied Daimler COG5 received a similar body from 1113 at the end of November 1948 before being sent for renovation at Samlesbury Engineering near Blackburn. Delicensed during 1954, it was one of forty-one COG5s put back into service 1958 and survived until May 1960. (L. Mason)

4477 (BJo3 EWH), waits in front of the Golden Hind Public House with its mock Tudor gable ends. The pub is on the corner of Greenholm Road and was opened on 18 November 1938, opposite a small row of shops in Kingstanding Road. In front of those shops is the modern bus shelter, more protective than had previously been the case on the Kingstanding Estate. One of the Line 33-dedicated Volvo B7TLs with Wright H46/26F bodies delivered in June 2003 is about to drop off a passenger on 9 July 2003. (D. R. Harvey)

This is roughly where Joe Tayman, an extremely experienced bus driver, was hit and killed by a passing Midland Counties milk lorry in 1952 as he stood talking to his changeover bus driver. 4299 (BU51 RYG) speeds down the hill in Kingstanding Road and is about to pass Tysoe Road, a cul-de-sac, on the right as it travels on its way into the city centre on the 33 route. This bus is a Volvo B7TL with an Alexander H47/27F body and entered service in February 2002. These bodies were also fitted to the contemporary Dennis Tridents. (D. R. Harvey)

When the 33 route was introduced to Ellerton Road by way of Newtown Row, Perry Barr and Kingstanding Road in August 1930, this was the first time that a bus service, rather than a tram route, had become the main public transport provider to a newly developed suburb; despite that, most of the route had either a central grass reservation or large tracts of open space alongside the carriageway. Bus 356 (OF 3988), was one of the dozen 338-367 class of petrol-engined AEC Regent 661s re-bodied by Brush with an MoS-style H30/21R body, in this case in September 1943. By 1949, because of their poor fuel economy and advancing years, these Birchfield Road garage-based buses were being restricted to peak-hour extras and shortworkings. No. 356 is heading towards Perry Barr on the 25 peak-hour service and is accelerating away from the last section of dual carriageway on the hill in Kingstanding Road at Crossway Lane. The 25 route was a peak-time service that left the Finchley Road terminus, which it shared with the 33 route to Kingstanding, and, on reaching Perry Barr, 'switched' routes and went via Villa Cross and Hockley into the city centre by way of the 29 route. To the right of the bus, the semi-detached houses are privately owned late-1920s properties. (D. Griffiths)

Above: Daimler Fleetline CRG6LX 3437 (437 KOV), has just turned into Kingstanding Road from College Road, which runs from right to left to New Oscott behind the bus. The open space behind the bus in College Road was the Joseph Lucas's sports ground, which always seemed to have immaculately prepared soccer pitches. Here, it has just arrived at the first bus stop in Kingstanding Road when working on the 33 route in around 1965. This was one of fifty Park Royal-bodied Fleetlines, which were something of a disappointment when first delivered, as unlike 3391–3400, bodied by Metro-Cammell with large 'V'-shaped windscreens, these buses, numbered 3401–3450, retained the original flat front design. (D. R. Harvey Collection)

Opposite above: Birmingham City Transport's first foray into two-door double-deckers were 100 vehicles introduced in 1968. These were the standard Daimler Fleetline CRG6LX model with Park Royal bodies, which in general outline looked like the previous fifty single-doored Park Royal bodies. The difference was that they had a nearside centre door and a staircase in the offside of the centre of the bus. The result was the loss of four seats in the lower saloon, giving them an H43/29D layout. 3802 (NOV 802G) was operating on the 90 route to the Pheasey Estate and is seen here travelling along Kingstanding Road near to Crossway Lane. Behind it are typical 1930s semi-detached privately built houses with bay windows, but without a side garage, which when new cost around £400. (D. R. Harvey Collection)

Opposite below: The first new buses used on the upgraded Line 33 were all but one of the first twenty of the 1997-built Volvo B10Ls with Wright B43F bodies, known by the type name of 'Liberator'. This design of Wright bodywork was specifically designed for low-floor buses with a flat front platform and access for wheelchairs and prams. 1415 (P415 EJW) slows down for the traffic lights at the junction with College Road on 22 February 1997. Until the 1960s this section of Kingstanding Road was two-way, with the semi-detached houses to the left standing around 30 yards back over a wide expanse of grass. This was subsequently torn up, and this section from College Road to Crossway Lane was rebuilt as a dual carriageway. On the right of the bus, the eastern side of the road was occupied by large semi-detached bungalows. Behind it is the long, straight route of Kingstanding Road, following the line of the Roman Ryknield Street, disappearing up the hill beyond the Golden Hind public house towards Hawthorn Road around a mile away. (D. R. Harvey)

The limited-stop 998 service to Kingstanding was introduced on 30 October 1977 as a replacement for the former 98 service when all the WMPTE limited-stop services were renumbered in the 9xx series. At the same time it was also extended along Kings Road to the Trees public house on Queslett Road. Having just turned into College Road from Kingstanding Road on 22 February 1997, 2282 (KJW 282W), a Mark I MCW Metrobus DR102/22 dating from June 1981, is just about to cross the bridge over the Birmingham Canal on its way towards the Boar's Head and the 13-acre Perry Park, opened in 1913 as an open space around a reservoir. The park was controlled by Perry Barr UDC but was taken over by the City of Birmingham in 1928, after which the swift construction of all the municipal housing in the Kingstanding area began. (D. R. Harvey)

Above: When the 29 bus route was originally introduced on 6 February 1928 as a cross-city service, it went from its southern terminus in Highfield Road, Hall Green, across the city and out to the north via Snow Hill, Summer Lane and Perry Barr. It carried on beyond the Perry Barr 6 route tram terminus to junction Aldridge Road with College Road at the 1930s-built Boar's Head public house opposite Perry Park. After the introduction of the new 33 route on 18 August 1930, the 29 route was extended from the Boar's Head up Kingstanding Road to terminate with the 33 in Ellerton Road. This arrangement was not satisfactory, as the northern end of the recently constructed Kingstanding beyond Hawthorn Road was not yet served by a bus route. As a result, the 29 route was diverted along the main road to Kingstanding Circle at Kings Road. The remnant of the use of the Boar's Head as the original terminus was that the 33A shortworking turned back in the triangle in front of the public house, in which 1707 (HOV 707), a Brush-bodied Leyland, stands in around 1951 with ALDRIDGE ROAD (BOAR'S HEAD) on the destination blind. (G. Davies)

Opposite below: Travelling out of the city, 3054 (MOF 54), a 1953-vintage Guy Arab IV with a Metro-Cammell H30/25R body, is working on the 90 route to Pheasey Estate. It is in College Road, and on the right in the distance is the Boar's Head public house, the location of the original terminus of the 29 route when it first opened on 6 February 1928. The bus is being followed by 3119 (MOF 119), a Crossley-bodied Daimler CVG6 that is also being employed on the 90 service. Behind the buses, on the skyline, is the section of the elevated M6 motorway between Gravelly Hill and Great Barr junctions. (D. R. Harvey Collection)

2140 (JOJ 140), speeds along Aldridge Road on its way back into Perry Barr on an inbound 29A service, having just crossed the River Tame. Again the houses were set back from the carriageway, suggesting that this was earmarked either for a tramway extension, for which Parliamentary Powers had been obtained, or more prosaically for future conversion into a dual carriageway. It was the latter that actually happened during the 1970s, some forty years after the road had been constructed! This Leyland Titan PD2/1 with a Leyland H30/26R body entered service on 25 March 1949 and was, along with 2142 and 2146, one of the last three of the type to remain in service, not being withdrawn until the last day of 1968. Unlike their pre-war TD6c equivalents, they had the normal Leyland 'L'-shaped staircase, despite Leyland Motors' offer to build the bodies with a standard BCT straight staircase for a small extra cost per bus. They also had the standard thin-backed Leyland seating with a Leyland-patterned, rather than BCT, moquette and were distinctly less comfortable to sit on during a long journey. (D. R. Harvey Collection)

Holford Drive to Birchfield
25, 29, 29A, 30, 33, 34, 90 and 91 routes

This was a most diverse section of all the routes and was centred on the important Perry Barr suburb which had been developed after the arrival of the railway in 1838. In the north off Aldridge Road was Holford Drive which led to the IMI Kynochs factory in Witton, but after 1947 a large tract of land was used by BCT to store withdrawn buses. Also, less than a quarter of a mile away was Wellhead Lane garage which had opened in 1932 with a capacity of around 160 buses. Opposite Wellhead Lane was the Alexander Stadium which was the original home of Birchfield Harriers and had been rebuilt in recent years as the Birmingham Brummies Speedway team. Perry Parr has been transformed by the development and subsequent economic benefit by the developing of the main Birmingham City University campus in Aldridge Road. At the junction of Aldridge Road and Walsall Road is the huge 1990s One Stop Shopping Centre which has reinvigorated Perry Barr which had become very run down since the opening of the very large underpass whose construction caused the demolition of many of the suburbs Victorian shops. Beyond the Witton Lane junction which had been the centre of Perry Barr's original shopping centre was Birchfield Road bus garage which had originally been opened as Birmingham Central Tramways steam tram depot on 25 November 1884. Towards Birmingham, Birchfield Road was a comparatively well-to-do area with behind the elaborate gate posts, walls and mature trees, large detached mid-nineteenth-century villas had been built, though most of these were lost when the Trinity Road was built in the 1960s.

An expanse of open ground off Holford Drive was used as a parking lot and dump for withdrawn Corporation buses between 1947 and 1955. Standing to the north of the Imperial Chemical Industries' huge ammunitions and metal industries factory and next to their Kynochs recreation club grounds off Aldridge Road, the site succeeded one on the corner of Western Road and Dudley Road. Virtually every type of pre-war bus, including Daimler COG5s, Leyland Titan TD6cs and wartime Guy Arabs and Daimler CWA6s, was taken to the site and stored until either sold to a breaker or to a dealer, who usually sold them on for further use. In 1954, the rows of some of the last buses to pass through the Holford Drive site show the variety of bus types being sold at this time. In the centre are 1110 (CVP 210), and 1025 (CVP 125), a pair of Metro-Cammell-bodied Daimler COG5s dating from 1937. On the left is 1269 (FOF 269), delivered in November 1939 as BCT's final COG5; this bus was re-bodied in August 1949 with one of the English Electric H28/26R bodies, built originally for Manchester Corporation. Across the puddles on the right is a Leyland-bodied Leyland Titan TD6c and behind that another of the same type, but like 1269, re-bodied with a Manchester-type English Electric body. (P. Tizard)

Perry Barr bus garage was opened in February 1932 and could lay claim at the time to having the largest unsupported bus garage roof in Europe. It was the largest bus garage in Birmingham with a maximum capacity of 160 vehicles. It initially operated the three cross-city services, the 5 and 7, the 15 and 16, the 29 and 29A, as well as the 33 and 34 and a share of operations on the Inner Circle 8 route and the Outer Circle 11. On 21 May 1932, through the main doorway of the garage is a pair of quite new AEC Regent 661s, with 426 (OG 426), a Vulcan-bodied vehicle, on the right and 454 (OV 4454), with a Short H27/21R body. Nearest the entrance is 203 (OP 232), an AEC 504 with a rare Birmingham-built Buckingham outside-staircase body, and on the extreme left is 115 (OM 214), a 1925 Short-bodied AEC 504. (First Leicester Archive)

A breakthrough as far as the Corporation was concerned was the purchase of 168 petrol-engined AEC Regent 661s. These all pioneered enclosed driver's cabs and enclosed straight staircase. Standing in Perry Barr yard in 1936 is 437 (OG 437), displaying the 29A route destination blind. This was one of thirty-five Regents that were bodied by Vulcan. It entered service on 18 October 1930 with a forty-eight-seat body with a piano front. This design was intended to reduce the weight over the front axle, but produced a rather ungainly front profile. As the Vulcan bodies were introduced before the Construction and Use Regulations of 1931, they did not have opening rear upper saloon emergency windows nor the 18-inch cut away on the back wall of the rear platform designed to allow passengers to crawl through the gap if the bus turned over on its nearside. Despite its apparently good condition, 437 would be withdrawn in July 1937 and sold for scrap. (BCT Official)

Perry Barr garage's original allocation of buses were AEC 504s, 507s and piano-fronted Regents, but these were joined in October and November 1933 by Metro-Cammell-bodied Morris-Commercial Imperial double-deckers 537–553 as well as the three Imperials with 'odd' bodies, specifically 504 (OC 504) with a Brush body, 505 (OC 505), with an English Electric body and 506 (OC 506), with a Gloucester RCW body. Parked in the yard when new are, from left to right, 551, 549, 539, 540, 547 and 543 (OC 551 etc.), with 540 displaying the destination blind for the 29 service. The gold lining-out on the fifty-seat bodywork enhances the sleek lines, which for the first time eliminated the piano front. The design of these bodies would be continued until the last pre-war deliveries of Daimler COG5s and Leyland Titan TD6cs. Unfortunately, the lightweight chassis of the Imperials were not so robust, with cracks occurring around the axles. Although the 7.698-litre petrol engines gave a good turn of speed, they tended to have a short crankshaft life, requiring constant retuning, and were characterised by more backfiring than on other petrol-engined types. In addition, the Imperials had an extremely short brake-pad life, a very awkward gearbox and the suspension gave a painfully bouncy and rough ride. As a result, these attractive buses had quite short lives, with 543 being withdrawn in December 1942 and 539 lasting until March 1946; the others went in either 1944 or 1945. (BCT Official)

Above: Travelling along Aldridge Road towards the city, with Perry Barr Stadium on the left and the main Birmingham City University campus on the bus's nearside, 4846 (BX61 LLT), is working on the 33 route on 23 February 2012. The bus is a Dennis Enviro 400 with an Alexander H45/32F body dating from 2011. The BCU had its origins in the City of Birmingham Polytechnic, set up in 1971 out of five long-established tertiary colleges elsewhere in the city. The latter's new Perry Barr campus became the centre of the new polytechnic, and in 1992 with a change in status it became University of Central England in Birmingham. In June 2007, UCE became Birmingham City University. The advantage to the National Express Group is that the numbers of students utilising the huge campus facilities mean an enormous increase in passengers using the 33 route. (D. R. Harvey)

Opposite above: On 1 July 1984, three of the same batch of Park Royal-bodied Leyland-engined Daimler Fleetlines, dating from February or March 1975, are parked inside Perry Barr garage. On the left is 4547, with 4538 in the centre and 4548 on the right. These GOG-N-registered buses were acquired with Leyland 0.680 engines, as there was a shortage of the more usual Gardner engines, and as a result sound more like Atlanteans than Fleetlines. These three buses were the last of the fifty to be converted to Gardner 6LXB engines between April and June 1986, a process which had begun in September 1980. 4530-4557 were allocated to Perry Barr, with the other half of the fifty going to Yardley Wood. (D. R. Harvey)

Opposite below: As the years went by, the destination display on the buses going to Collingwood Drive was gradually reduced to the word PHEASEY, which was almost as unhelpful as the old CITY display. Volvo B10L 1407 (P407 EJW), with the Line 33-dedicated route livery, passes the Perry Barr Stadium on 21 July 1997. The stadium was originally constructed for Birchfield Harriers, who held its opening ceremony on 27 July 1929. The facade still carries their badge, a running stag in an Art deco-style bas relief. Birchfield Cycling Club used the venue for cycle races, and in the mid-1930s the cycle track outside the running lanes was used for dirt-track speedway racing. In the Second World War, the stadium was requisitioned and used by the Home Guard. Used to accommodate Italian prisoners of war until January 1946, Birchfield Harriers returned to the stadium the following month. On Saturday evenings the stadium was hired out to Birmingham Speedway. Floodlighting was installed to facilitate the latter and this allowed for the first floodlit athletics meeting ever held in the United Kingdom, in September 1948. In their centenary year in 1977, Birchfield Harriers moved to the newly built Alexander Stadium nearby, as it was then renamed. Since 1990 the Perry Barr Stadium has been used for greyhound racing, succeeding, some six years after demolition, the old Perry Barr dog track, which stood roughly where the present-day One Stop shopping centre is now located. Since 1997 speedway has returned to the Perry Barr Stadium, as it is the home of the Birmingham Brummies speedway team. (D. R. Harvey)

Above: Looking towards Aldridge Road from the Aston Lane junction in September 1960, all traces of the tram tracks have long since disappeared, though otherwise little had changed since the demise of the 6 tram route at the end of 1949. On the right, next to the parked early post-war Austin 8 van, is the New Crown & Cushion. 1518 (GOE 518), a 1947 Daimler CVA6 with a MCCW body, is approaching the entrance to Perry Barr railway station when working on an outbound 29 service. Although rebuilt around the time of electrification in the 1960s, this station stands on the site of the original Grand Junction railway station of 1838 and is the oldest station on its original site in Birmingham and one of the oldest continually operated station sites in the world! All the buildings on the left were demolished within the next few years in order to accommodate the new Perry Barr underpass. In the distance is the large roof of Franchise Street School and the tower of the by-then-deconsecrated Christ Church, which stood in the angle of Aldridge Road and Walsall Road, though by this time it was being used as a large carpenter's woodyard and sawmill. (Commercial postcard)

Opposite above: About to turn underneath the Perry Barr flyover in Walsall Road in early West Midland PTE days is 3134 (MOF 134). This Crossley-bodied Daimler CVG6 is working on the northbound 90 service to Pheasey, and once beyond the concrete overbridge it will turn left into Aldridge Road. Behind the bus is the original mid-1960s Perry Barr shopping precinct, which was replaced in the 1990s by the One Stop shopping centre. 3134, which entered service on 1 September 1953, was to have a very long life, as it was only withdrawn when the last BCT Standards were taken out of service on 31 October 1977. (D. R. Harvey Collection)

Opposite below: Standing in the terminal track stub in around 1947 outside the New Crown & Cushion public house in Perry Barr is UEC-bodied tram 17. The tram has yet to be painted in the post-war livery. Dated from January 1904 as an open topper, car 17 was fitted with a top cover in July 1907. It was re-bogied with EMB Burnley bogies in 1924 as well being re-motored with DK 30B 40-hp motors and having the vestibules enclosed. Known as the 'Aston bogies', the I-20 class spent over twenty-five years working on the 6 route to Perry Barr, and although fourteen of the class were destroyed due to enemy action in the Second World War, car 17 would soldier on until 31 December 1949, when the route was withdrawn. Overtaking the tram on its nearside is an EHA-registered Brush-bodied SOS FEDD still in its pre-war livery. Behind the tram and the Midland Red bus near to the railway bridge at Perry Barr railway station is a BCT Daimler COG5 with a BRCW body, working its way into the city on a 29A duty. (D. R. Harvey Collection)

Above: Perry Barr underpass in Birchfield Road was opened early in 1962. On 31 May 1962, with the demolition of the Victorian premises near Witton Lane all but completed, the sheer size of the underpass can be appreciated. It was one of the first such schemes to be built in an urban area in Britain and took traffic on the A34 out of the increasingly bad rush hour congestion that was beginning to blight Perry Barr. As if to contradict the improvements made to speed up the traffic, passing towards is a hearse and three funeral cars on their way to Perry Barr crematorium in nearby Walsall Road. Travelling into the city is 3138 (MOF 138), a 1953-vintage Crossley-bodied Daimler CVG6, while at the traffic underpass island is a Midland Red D9 double-decker coming into the city from Sutton Coldfield. In the foreground is the former Birchfield Road garage entrance, which due to the road-widening scheme was closed and a new entrance built 'round the back' in Leslie Road. (BC Ref. Library)

Opposite above: Working on an inbound 29 route on 8 August 1967, only six months before it was taken out of service, is one of Hockley garage's Leyland-bodied Leyland Titan PD2/1s. 2166 (JOJ 166) negotiates the traffic island over the Perry Barr underpass. The large Victorian Perry Barr Methodist church with the Outer Circle 11 bus stop in front of it looms large over Witton Lane as a Vauxhall Victor FB estate car turns onto the traffic island. 2166 was one of twenty-eight of the class to have entered service during May 1949. These Leyland-bodied Leyland Titan PD2/1s were bought virtually 'off the peg' after Brush could not meet delivery dates for the second half of their order. Being some 6 inches lower than the standard BCT bus, some were operated on the 2B route between Kings Heath and the Ivy Bush, since in Dads Lane, Kings Heath, there was a low bridge that would just accommodate them. Alas, the roadway was lowered just before their delivery began! (J. Carroll)

Opposite below: In around 1959, 3108 (MOF 108), a Crossley-bodied Daimler CVG6, travels into the city when working on a CITY service, hence the blank rear destination number box. It entered service for the final Miller Street tram conversion in July 1953. Another of the same type is on the forecourt of Birchfield Road garage and is about to turn into Birchfield Road. 3108 is about to pass 1590 (GOE 590), a Daimler CVG6 working on an outbound 33 route. Passing the Birchfield Cinema is Crossley-bodied Crossley DD42/6, also employed on the 33 service. The vehicles in the foreground are all Fords, with the roof of an almost new Zephyr II visible, followed by a Fordson E83W van, a Popular 103G and a top-of-the-range Zodiac Mark I EOTTA. The buildings on the left side of Birchfield Road between Witton Lane and Bragg Road were pulled down in order to accommodate the road-widening scheme, which included the Perry Barr underpass. (D. R. Harvey Collection)

Towards the end of 1950, all of the surviving re-bodied 7.4-litre petrol-engined AEC Regent 661s had congregated at Birchfield Road garage as this was the last garage to have petrol tanks and pumps and was regarded as the 'home of geriatric buses'. New Year's Eve 1950 was the final day of BCT's operation of petrol-engined buses. The very last journey of all was undertaken by 338 (OG 3638). The bus is posed with its driver and two fitters just inside the entrance to Birchfield Road garage. 338 was an AEC Regent 661 whose chassis replaced the original 1929 prototype chassis of 338 during the following year but reused the original Brush body. The bus was re-bodied by the same coachbuilder in 1944 but with an angled staircase, giving it three more seats, at fifty-four, than those of the fifty re-bodies fitted with straight staircases. (*Birmingham Evening Despatch*)

Above: Parked near to the entrance of Birchfield Road garage is another of the MoS-style Brush-re-bodied petrol-engined AEC Regent 661s. 358's chassis dated from December 1929, but was deemed good enough to be re-bodied by Brush, re-entering service in March 1944, but with an angled rather than straight staircase, which increased its seating capacity by three in the lower saloon to H30/24R. These AEC re-bodies were used sparingly after around 1947, usually on peak-hour extras. The conductress sits on the lower saloon's long back seat awaiting her driver to turn the bus around and begin another trip back to Birmingham. 358, although withdrawn two months before the last of these elderly buses, was one of the last survivors, being used by the London Brick Company of Stewartby as a staff bus until April 1956. (P. M. Photography)

Opposite below: The transient nature of the vehicles allocated to Birchfield Road garage is well exemplified here, as none of the buses in the garage here on 13 July 1952 were there in 1950 and only the trio of Daimler CVA6s were at the garage in 1954. The identifiable MCCW-bodied Daimler COG5s are 1146 (FOF 146), 1123 (CVP 223), 1230 (FOF 230), and 1008 (CVP 108), with Daimler CVA6 1493 (GOE 493) being the first of the identifiable post-war buses. Opened originally in November 1884 as a small six-track steam-tram depot for Birmingham Central Tramways, Birchfield Road was acquired by BCT on the closure of the Perry Barr steam-tram service on New Years' Eve 1906 and was reopened on 2 May 1907 as an electrified tram depot with a capacity for around twenty trams, used as mainly peak-hour extras on the Perry Barr service and to provide extras on Villa Park specials. It was finally closed for trams on 3 October 1924 and reopened as a bus garage on 28 October the following year. In the 1920s and 30s Birchfield Road garage was opened and closed no less than three times but became a permanent overspill garage on 18 November 1940 for Perry Barr until it was finally closed on 20 August 1966. (D. R. Harvey Collection)

Above: Loading up with passengers in Birchfield Road at the Thornbury Road red tram stop is tramcar 8. This tram has just left the distant 6 route Perry Barr terminus and was one of the six survivors of the original open-top ER&TCW-bodied Corporation bogie tramcars built in January 1904. The tram was withdrawn in October 1949 after being involved in an accident. Behind the tram and just passing the Birchfield Cinema is a 1948-vintage Brush-bodied Leyland PD2/1 which is on the 29A route. The Birchfield Cinema opened on 25 September 1913 as the Birchfield Picturedrome and seated 930 people. Its other claim to fame was that it was one of the first suburban cinemas in the city to be fitted with a CinemaScope screen. It was closed on 3 March 1962 with a final showing of *South Pacific.* Just visible is a petrol-engined AEC Regent with a wartime Brush body turning out of Aston Lane. (D. R. Harvey Collection)

Opposite above: Coming into Perry Barr along Birchfield Road during 1959 is Pheasey Estate-bound 1122 (CVP 222). This Daimler COG5 is working on the 29A route passing Willmore Road, some road widening for a new bus stop and the row of shops just before Birchfield Road bus garage, which was at this time the home of 1122. It had entered service on 9 November 1937 and, unusually, survived without being involved in the early post-war body swaps, to be one of ninety bus bodies renovated by Samlesbury Engineering, re-entering service in February 1948. The bus was licensed as Liverpool Street garage's snowplough from November 1954 until 30 April 1958, whereupon it was sent to Tyburn Road works, overhauled and returned to service on 1 September 1958. Having had a considerable amount of money spent on its overhaul and refurbishment, it was only back in use for a little over two years as one of the last of the forty-one reinstated COG5s being withdrawn on New Year's Eve 1960. (L. Mason)

Opposite below: A well-laden 'New Look'-front Daimler CVD6 stands in the bus lay-by in Birchfield Road between Bragg Road and the Broadway in around 1958. 2105 (JOJ 105) entered service on 1 June 1951 from Perry Barr garage and spent the next twelve years based there. It is working on the 29A route to Baldwins Lane. The bus stands outside the Wellington Radio and Electric shop with one of the 'newfangled' television sets in their window. Behind the Daimler is a branch of Lloyds Bank and Joseph Harris, the Birmingham-based dry cleaners. (R. H. G. Simpson)

On the day after Birmingham City Transport had been taken over by West Midland PTE, ten-month-old, dual-doored Park Royal-bodied Daimler Fleetline CRG6LX 3806 (NOV 806G) travels away from Perry Barr along Birchfield Road towards Trinity Church. Within two years this scene would be unrecognisable as the road would become a six-way dual carriageway and this point would mark the beginning of the Trinity Road flyover. The bus is working on the 34 route to Quinton. (D. R. Harvey Collection)

In 1949, standing behind tram 8 is Metro-Cammell H30/24R-bodied 1603 (GOE 603). This Daimler CVG6 is about to turn right into Heathfield Road when working on the 29 route and has its illuminated trafficator arm extended. The tram will carry straight on along Birchfield Road towards Six Ways, Aston and Newtown Row. Today, this is the site of the Trinity Road flyover, whose construction was completed in 1970. Noticeably, the tramcar is adorned with a large number of advertisements but the bus has none, as it was the policy of the Transport Department not to have any until around May 1953, when the contracts for the trams expired. (R. T. Wilson)

Six Ways, Aston to Lancaster Place

This section briefly deals with the 33 route.

The 33 bus route continued along Birchfield Road to Six Ways, Aston. This important junction had another shopping area clustered around it. Yet Alma Street and its continuation into Summer Lane was of the most notorious areas in Birmingham for hard-living 'Brummies' with a pub on every corner and a fight every Friday night in most of the pubs. In the Summer Lane area, Lozells and Wheeler Street were some of the most tightly-packed back-to-back courtyards in Birmingham all dating from before they were made illegal by the Housing Act of 1874. The area of Newtown was just that, a 'New Town' when it was developed by Aston Council in the 1840s. Running through the middle of it was Newtown Row, which later formed part of the main A34 road from the edge of the city to virtually Six Ways. The area was an important, thriving suburb with a large number of privately owned shops; it also had its own theatre, the Aston Hippodrome, its own department store, the House That Jack Built, one of the best known Victorial public houses in Birmingham, the Barton's Arms and much industry. Nearly all of these were swept away in the 1960s and 1970s when road developments tore a swathe of dual carriageway through the area.

Crossing the junction at Six Ways, Aston, is tramcar 451 on its way to Perry Barr on the 6 route. It is being followed by an Austin K3 lorry and an Austin 30 cwt Three-Way van. On the right is the Ansells-Brewery-owned Royal Exchange public house standing on the corner of Alma Street, while coming out of Victoria Road is an Austin Sixteen car, dating from June 1947. Alma Street was the route taken by the 33 bus service from its instigation until it was diverted via High Street and Newtown Row in January 1950. Behind it is the large Dutch-gabled premises of the National Provincial Bank dating from 1900. Car 451 was the first of three open-top trams built with five-bay bodies by the company at Kyotts Lake Road works in 1903 as CBT 178. Two of the three were taken over by BCT in July 1911. At 34 feet 8 inches long they were the longest trams operated by the Corporation and were the only ones of five-bay construction and rebuilt with top covers and DK13A 40 hp motors by 1926. They were nicknamed the 'Titanics' on account of their size and, along with the six 'Aston' bogies that survived the war, continued to work from Miller Street until the Perry Barr tram route was closed on 31 December 1949. (W. A. Camwell)

Alma Street got its name from the Battle of Alma, which took place during the Crimean War, on 20 September 1854. The 33 bus route to Kingstanding went to the city centre by way of Six Ways, Aston Alma Street and Summer Lane. When the Perry Barr tramway route was abandoned on New Year's Eve 1949, the 33 was diverted from the former route to get into the city by way of Newtown Row. 1719 (HOV 719) has just passed into Alma Street from Six Ways, with the Royal Exchange public house behind it on 15 December 1949, just a fortnight before the rerouting. Parked on the left is a Middlesex-registered 1935 Chrysler DeLuxe Eight. By this time Alma Street had some pretty appalling back-to-back courtyards, such as Myrtle, Victoria, Builth and Roslin Places. Despite their attractive names they were dingy and unhealthy brick-floored courtyards with communal outside lavatories and criss-crossed by washing lines. (G. F. Douglas courtesy of A. D. Packer)

Travelling towards Six Ways along Newtown Row near Lower Tower Street are two buses operating on the 33 route to Kingstanding. The buildings along this section of Newtown Row were already derelict and awaiting demolition. The only identifiable building is one last occupied by Frank Ash, who had advertised his business as 'The Noted Bacon Shop'. After the Perry Barr tramway route was abandoned, the 33 bus route was diverted from the former route by way of Newtown Row. The leading bus is 2128 (JOJ 128), a 1951 'New Look'-front Daimler CD6-engined Daimler CVD6 with a Metro-Cammell body. It has just overtaken a parked 1956 Standard Vanguard III and is being followed by a Triumph Herald convertible. Behind the Daimler bus is the three-years-older 1701 (HOV 701), a well-laden Brush-bodied Leyland Titan PD2/1 which was eventually withdrawn in November 1968. It would appear that the Leyland's driver has done all the hard work from the city centre and has been overtaken by the nearly empty 2128. Both buses were allocated to Perry Barr garage. (D. R. Harvey Collection)

Above: Going towards the city is one of the attractively fronted MCCW Daimler Fleetline CRG6LXs. Even the small TO CITY blind is set correctly. 3395 (395 KOV), allocated to Perry Barr garage, is around a year old and is working on an inbound 33 service. The bus has just passed the Municipal Bank near Manchester Street in Newtown Row. Although the shops on the right have later Victorian frontal extensions, closer examination shows that their upper storeys dated from around the 1830s, which is when the 'new town' area of Aston was first developed. All this was swept away in the 1970s when the Newtown redevelopment involved cutting a swathe of a dual carriageway from the Inner Ring Road to Great Barr. (S. N. J. White)

Opposite above: The half-price footwear for sale at N. B. Shoes, on the corner of Inkerman Street and High Street, Newtown, Aston, appears to be creating some interest as groups of people do their shopping one Saturday morning in November 1949. Car 581 is working the 6 route and is on a short section of interlaced track in front of The House That Jack Built store, beyond the shoppers to the right. This was one of the first independent suburban department stores. The tram is just above the culverted Hockley Brook, a tributary of the River Tame, which in medieval times had been a problem to cross. Tram 581 entered service in February 1914 and was briefly used on the short-lived 'First Class' experiment along the recently opened Hagley Road route. Behind the tramcar is the famous Aston Hippodrome, which was opened to the public on 7 December 1908 at a cost of £10,000. Performances were held twice daily, and over the years many famous stars appeared here, including Wee Georgie Wood, George Robey, George Formby, Sid Fields, Ted Ray, Sandy Powell, Will Hay, Laurel and Hardy (in one of their last appearances in the UK, in May 1954, before their final tour was cut short because of Oliver Hardy's poor health), Gracie Fields, Larry Grayson, Morecambe and Wise and Judy Garland. On 4 June 1960, it closed as a theatre and was converted into a bingo hall and remained so until its demolition in September 1980. (F. L. Jones)

Having been hit by a crane in Newtown Row on 1 November 1960, 3130 (MOF 130), a 1953 Daimler CVG6, stands forlornly awaiting its fate. The accident damage ripped out most of the nearside upper deck, causing major structural damage to the Crossley body. Inside the top deck are two officials from the Transport Department who are inspecting the appalling destruction. The bus would be driven to Tyburn Road works to be completely rebuilt, and would be back in service within months. Despite this damage, the bus would survive into West Midlands PTE days and was not withdrawn until July 1975. (D. R. Harvey Collection)

Not long before Newtown Row was rebuilt as a six-lane dual carriageway, 2677 (A677 UOE), a MCW Metrobus Mark II DR102/27 with an MCW H43/30F body, is about to cross the Middle Ring Road at New John Street West on 12 October 1984. The Mark II model was introduced in May 1982 and had a more pleasing frontal appearance than the Mark I with a deep windscreen. 2677 entered service in September 1983 and is working on an outbound 33 service to Finchley Road. It is being followed by another Mark II Metrobus, 2507 (POG 507Y), working on the 51 route to the Beeches Estate. (D. R. Harvey)

One of the most enjoyable, exciting rides on a Birmingham bus was to go over the Birmingham-Fazeley Canal bridge in Newtown Row. This was akin to riding over the top of a fairground big dipper, only one could do it in both directions. 3272 (272 GON), is leaving the city centre on the 33 route on 4 July 1971 when in WMPTE ownership and is about to crest the 'hump' of the bridge. This Park Royal-bodied Daimler Fleetline CRG6LX entered service on 1 September 1963 as one of the first production batch of BCT rear-engined buses. On the other side of the road on the crest of the bridge there was a cast-iron urinal, which, being directly over the canal, always seemed to be in an ideal location! (J. Carroll)

Emerging from Lancaster Street into Lancaster Place on 13 October 1964 is sixteen-year-old Brush-bodied Leyland Titan PD2/1 1729 (HOV 729). 1729 is working on an inbound 33 service to Union Street. In front of the bus is Birmingham's Central Fire Station, while dominating Lancaster Place is the large 1960s-built offices and warehousing of Halford's Cycle Company, the bicycle and car accessory manufacturer. Their original warehouse had been replaced after a somewhat embarrassing event, as it caught fire on 12 March 1955, right under the noses of the city's Fire Brigade! By the time a passer-by had noticed that the old building's bricks were red hot, it was too late and it was a total loss! At the time it was the largest fire in the city since the wartime bombing raids of 1940 and 1941. (W. Ryan)

Heathfield Road; Lozells and Hockley to Constitution Hill
25, 29, 29A, 30, 90 and 91 routes

The area from Heathfield Road, through to the shopping centre in Lozells Road around Villa Cross and beyond to Hamstead Road was a well-to-do area of mainly large Victorian villas and semi-detached houses, although there were a number of rows of Regency properties in the suburb. The thriving shops in Villa Road were served by the intersuburban number 5 tram service. At Hamstead Road the cross-city 16 bus service from Hamstead in the north to Yardley in the south side of the City came over Villa Road. The 29 group of routes turned into Hamstead Road vefore reaching Soho Hill where the route descended into the shopping centre of Hockley. THis was another shopping centre but which was totally removed when the Hockley Flyover was built in the mid-1960s. This was where the Inner Circle, 8 bus route crossed the main A41 and where the Corporation bus garage in Whitmore Street was located. This was originally the former Birmingham Central Tramways cable-car dept and was used until 2008 by the National Express West Midlands. The route then climbed towards the city up Hockley Hill with the large Joseph Lucas factory to the east of the main route while to the west the routes skirted Birmingham's famous Jewellery Quarter before arriving at Constitution Hill.

Waiting at the traffic lights in Heathfield Road, at the junction with Birchfield Road, is 2179 (JOJ 179). It is working on an outbound 90 service to Pheasey in around 1967. The trees and the by-now grass-covered open space on the corner of Heathfield Road were swept away some three years later when the Trinity Road flyover was built over this junction. This was the penultimate vehicle in the batch of fifty Leyland Titan PD2/1s with Leyland H30/26R bodies which had entered service in 1949. Behind the bus is a Ford Anglia 105E, a Bedford CA van and Bedford and Ford Thames tippers. (D. F. Potter)

Above: As late as 1950, petrol-engined AEC Regent 661s could still be seen working on all-day duties. Going home from work with his coat over his arm, a passenger hangs on to the platform stanchion of 470 as it turns into Villa Road from Hamstead Road on Friday 16 June 1950. Dating from September 1931, OV 4470 was re-bodied with a MoS Brush H30/21R body, re-entering service in December 1943. These wartime re-bodies were only completed as a shell reusing all the old body parts such as the seats, light and bell fixtures and in this case the straight staircase, which was not found on regular 'utility' bodies. It is working on the 29A route from Baldwins Lane, Hall Green, to Pheasey Estate. In front of Francis Hallam's dispensing chemist shop is a 1920 Brush-bodied bogie tram, 589, working on the inter-suburban 5 tram route between Lozells and Gravelly Hill. A Daimler CVD6, working on the 29 route, is carrying a radiator slip-board reading BULL RING, suggesting that it would turn back once it had reached High Street. (G. F. Douglas courtesy A. D. Packer)

Opposite above: Daimler CVA6 1526 (GOE526) climbs up Heathfield Road when on its way towards Villa Cross in around 1963. The bus is working on the 91 service and is displaying the blind showing HALL GREEN BALDWINS LANE. Heathfield Road, which got its name from Heathfield House, built in 1790 and occupied variously by industrialists James Watt and George Tangye, was lined with large, late nineteenth-century semi-detached villas, showing that when they were built this was a most prestigious residential area, lying between Birchfield and Lozells. Since the 90 stopped being a cross-city bus route, Heathfield Road has been served by the 46 bus. (R. Beesley)

Opposite below: Turning into Villa Road from Heathfield Road on a 92 service is 2862 (JOJ 862). In the apex of these two roads is the Villa Cross public house. This Ansells pub dated from the 1920s, having replaced an eighteenth-century three-storeyed inn. On a miserable evening in around 1970, the Daimler CVG6's driver has switched on the interior saloon lights while the Belisha Beacon is shining brightly as it flashes on and off. The bus is fitted with one of the BCT replacement mesh radiator grills, which looked quite awful. (G. Barnes)

Above: Still painted in full BCT livery but with vinyl WM fleet name stickers, 3131 (MOF 131), a 1953 Daimler CVG6 with a Crossley H30/25R body, works on a city-bound 90 service on Friday 19 June 1970. It stands on Soho Hill just below the large white-fronted former New Palladium Cinema, which opened in this style in 1927 with a seating capacity of 841 and closed on 13 February 1965, though it subsequently survived as a bingo hall and a retail warehouse for nearly another forty years. (P. Yeomans)

Opposite above: In 1938, bus 402 (OG 402), an AEC Regent 661 with an English Electric piano-front-style body, has just turned out of Villa Road and is standing outside the Baptist church in Hamstead Road, built in 1883. 402 entered service on 1 December 1930 and was soon allocated to Perry Barr garage after the latter establishment's opening in 1932. It was re-bodied with a Brush MoS-style replacement, re-entering service on Bonfire Night 1943, and was withdrawn in 1950. (R. T. Coxon)

Opposite below: During the construction of the Hockley flyover in 1966, the route of the carriageway was altered in order that the flow of traffic was not disturbed by the construction. On the distant corner of Hamstead Road and Soho Hill is the Roebuck Public House and it is from Hamstead Road that Crossley-bodied Daimler CVG6 2882 (JOJ 882) has come onto the start of the Hockley flyover construction works. The construction of the enormously complex Hockley flyover scheme of the late 1960s involved the demolition of all the large Victorian semi-detached houses on the western side of Soho Hill. By this time, the wasteland caused by the road widening ended at the junction with Richmond Road beyond the Ford Popular 103G. (R. H. G. Simpson)

After entering service on 1 July 1948, just a year later, MCCW-bodied Daimler CVD6 1803 (HOV 803) was reintroduced on 8 July 1949 with the proposed design for the triple indicator display boxes that were to be introduced on the 'New Look'-front buses whose delivery was to begin during the following year. As a result the bus spent the next few years wandering around various garages so that conducting crews could become familiar with the new design. It always looked slightly peculiar, an 'odd bus out', being the only exposed-radiator double-decker in the fleet with triple destination indicator, and was one of the first of the class to be withdrawn in August 1963. It is seen on an inbound 29A service and is passing through Hockley Brook in around 1959, having descended Soho Hill, where the large three-storey shops have their sunblinds pulled down. The bus is about to pull away from the stop where the CBT cable trams, abandoned in 1911, had to coast across the gap between the inner cable from Colmore Row and the outer cable to the New Inns in Handsworth. (R. H. G. Simpson)

Above: Whitmore Street was built in 1888 as Birmingham Central Tramway's depot for their cable-car service, which housed all fifty-three cable trams. This was operated from Colmore Row to Hockley Brook on 24 March 1888 and was extended on a second cable to the New Inns, Handsworth, on 21 April 1889. When the original twenty-one-year lease expired on 30 June 1911, it was closed for conversion to the new Corporation electric trams, being reopened on 12 June 1912. In the foreground are the remnants of the depot's tram tracks, which survived the conversion to buses on 1 April 1939. On the night of 22/23 November 1940, the recently converted Hockley bus garage was bombed, resulting in nineteen buses being burnt out, yet only six buses were written off as destroyed and twelve re-bodied. On its conversion to buses, Hockley's original 1939 fleet was made up of Leyland-bodied Titan TD6cs with MCCW bodies. By 1950, the garage had been re-equipped with the whole batch of fifty Leyland-bodied PD2/1s and fifteen PD2/1s with stylish Park Royal bodywork. In 1965, 2158 (JOJ 158), one of the former vehicles, stands on the forecourt of Hockley garage with blinds set for the 90 route, a route numbering which had replaced the 29A on 29 November 1964. Hockley garage finally closed in May 2005 though the original 1888 building is listed. (R. Duke)

Opposite below: New to Perry Barr garage in October 1964, 3445 (445 KOV) has just rounded Hockley Circus beneath Hockley flyover and has passed the entrance into Hockley garage. It is climbing Soho Hill alongside the flyover when working on a 90 service to Pheasey. This Daimler Fleetline CRG6LX has a Park Royal body which when built was a seventy-two seater but was given an extra row of seats in the upper saloon in September 1969, just before the PTE takeover. The bus had been converted to OMO in 1973 and carries the blank plate to show that it is not working as a one-man bus. The 90 service was not converted to driver-only use until 1 June 1975 and is using a conductor who is standing on the platform. 3445 did not last long enough to be involved in this as it was the first of these buses to be withdrawn – during 1974, having been involved in an accident. (R. Weaver)

Above: At first sight looking like an ordinary 29 service, a well-laden 428 (OG 428) is actually working on a Lucas Works special in Great King Street, which it is leaving at the end of a shift. On the radiator is a slip board revealing that the bus is on its way to Kingstanding. The cars overtaking the bus are a Morris Eight Series I saloon dating from around 1936 and a Ford CX Fordor saloon. The Corporation bus is an AEC Regent 661 with a Vulcan H27/21R which dated from July 1930. Unlike other members of the batch, this one was never altered during the war and it was withdrawn on Leap Year Day 1944. (D. R. Harvey Collection)

Opposite above: Passing through Hockley Brook in around 1960 is 1490 (GOE 490). It is working on the 29 route to Highfield Road, Hall Green. The bus was one of the first post-war double-deckers to be delivered to BCT and entered service on 18 July 1947. Hockley had a thriving, if somewhat run-down, late Victorian shopping centre, which included the Birmingham Municipal Bank on the corner of Farm Street. Next to the bus is Frederick Higgs tobacconist's shop. Behind the bus is a Vauxhall Victor Series II while opposite is one of the great disasters of the British motor industry, the Austin Atlantic A90 saloon, in this case registered by Worcester CC in January 1951. (F. W. York)

Opposite below: Climbing up Hockley Hill is one of the last Birmingham Standards that entered service in October 1954, 3224 (MOF 224). This is a Crossley-bodied Daimler CVG6 and is approaching Key Hill in around 1959 when working on the long 29A service to Baldwins Lane. It is passing the booking office of Frames Tours, a well-known Birmingham coach-tour operator. Next door is an 1890s building with multicoloured brickwork frontage which contains workshops of silversmiths Gloster Joseph, and next door Britton & Son who were goldsmiths. These premises marked the edge of the Jewellery Quarter. (L. Mason)

On 9 October 1979, Metro-Cammell-bodied Daimler Fleetline CRG6LX 4233 (YOX 233K), which entered service in July 1972, travels into the city along Great Hampton Street, near to the Jewellery Quarter in Hockley. It is working on the 90 route to Baldwins Lane. The building behind the bus on the west side of Great Hampton Street is the large 1890s Great Hampton Street works, which had formerly been multi-occupied by Charles Cooper, a manufacturer of rolling mill machinery; Hathaway & Muddiman, ringmakers; and, coincidentally, a radio wholesaler who was also named Hathaway! Next door, behind the Commer lorry, is a row of original Regency houses which lined the street. These houses were built in 1830 and became workshops for no less than five small companies. In 1997, the Birmingham Conservation Trust restored these two properties to their original condition. (F. W. York)

Around the City Centre

Constitution Hill– Snow Hill
25, 29, 29A, 30, 90 and 91 routes

This short section between the edge of Hockley and the city centre in Snow Hill was dominated on the western side by the Great Western Railway's Snow Hill Station and the bridges, viaducts and the railway accoutrements to the north of the station. The route of the 29 group of services was joined by the 5 route at the junction with Summer Lane and just before the dominating twin towers of St Chad's Roman Catholic Cathedral. The old Snow Hill led up to the junction with Colmore Row and Steelhouse Lane and yet again the road was obliterated when Snow Hill Ringway was built in the 1970s, later to be renamed Snow Hill Queensway when HM the Queen opened the last section of the Inner Ring Road and in error referred to the complete road as 'The Queensway' rather than the section she was opening. Birmingham Council then felt honour-bound to rename all the roads and so Snow Hill Ringway became Snow Hill Queensway.

Passing the Downtown Warehouse as it pulls away from the bus stop in Constitution Hill is 6961 (WDA 961T). This Leyland Fleetline FE30AGR had an MCW H43/33F body and entered service in November 1978. In April 1990 the bus is travelling on an outwards journey on the 91 service with just the brief destinations of PHEASEY VIA HOCKLEY on the front blinds. Behind the bus is the YMCA building and beyond is St Chad's Circus. (D. R. Harvey)

Above: Turning out of Snow Hill and into Steelhouse Lane is a newly overhauled 1751 (HOV 751). This Brush-bodied Leyland Titan PD2/1 looks in pristine condition as it travels in a somewhat circuitous route to its terminus in High Street, as it is working on the CITY shortworking from Kingstanding Circle. The bus is carrying an advertisement for Fox's Biscuits, a confectioner famous for their ginger nuts; the company was founded in Batley in 1853 and is still in business at the time of writing. This important shopping area was totally swept away in the early 1960s in order to accommodate the Inner Ring Road scheme at a time when the city planners were concerned with traffic schemes which favoured motorists over pedestrians and shoppers. (D. R. Harvey Collection)

Opposite above: The original line of Snow Hill was lost when Snow Hill Ringway was opened in 1964 and linked St Chad's Circus with Colmore Circus. In the new ringway, Metro-Cammell-bodied Daimler CVD6 2723 (JOJ 723), new in October 1951, pulls away from the stop when being employed on the 29 route. The bodies on these 150 buses were the first built for BCT with one-piece metal-framed bodies, which made them easily identifiable by not having the between-decks guttering found on all the earlier buses that were traditionally built in two halves. Alongside the bus is Lloyd House, which was opened in 1963. Most of the building was occupied by the then Birmingham City Police as their headquarters while almost hidden on the right was The Carousel restaurant and steak bar. (D. R. Harvey Collection)

Opposite below: The inbound 29 and 29A bus service first made contact with the city centre at the top of the old Snow Hill. By 1962, the area was in terminal decline due to the expiry of leases and the serving of compulsory purchase orders on the Victorian properties opposite the railway station. The premises of Samuel Thornley, who sold paints, oils and chemicals, a trade that was known as a drysalting, has a sign in the window showing that due to the impending construction of the Inner Ring Road, they had moved to Newtown Row. John Hall's tool merchant has also recently been closed down, and the wines and spirits merchant's shop formerly owned by T. Foster has actually been partially demolished. Waiting to pull away from the bus stop barriers outside these doomed buildings is bus 2097 (JOJ 97), one of Yardley Wood garage's Daimler CVD6s dating from March 1951. (R. H. G. Simpson)

Above: Perry Barr garage only rarely had any of the exposed-radiator HOV-registered Daimler CVG6s allocated to it but after Highgate Road garage closed in July 1962 a few of the earlier buses did spend a short period of time working from there. 1849 (HOV 849) is passing the new home of the *Birmingham Post* and *Evening Mail* newspapers. This complex, between Colmore Circus and Printing House Street, was begun in 1963 to a design of J. H. D. Madin & Partners and consisted of a main block of four storeys surmounted by a sixteen-storey tower block of offices faced in marble, black granite and stone; it was officially opened by HRH Princess Margaret on 26 October 1965. (PhotoFives)

Opposite above: The very first post-war BCT bus was Daimler CVA6 1481 (GOE 481). It is working on CITY service to High Street. On 1 June 1959 this Metro-Cammell-bodied bus has just passed the Gaumont Cinema in Steelhouse Lane with beyond that the corner of Slaney Street and the George & Dragon public house. All of this area was demolished when Colmore Circus was redeveloped in 1964. On the extreme left is the main branch of Harrisons optician's, which stood on the corner of Snow Hill and was one of twenty branches in Birmingham. Next door, in Steelhouse Lane, beneath its extended canvas sunblind, Finlay's tobacconist shop is doing good business selling their smoking requisites, perhaps including the popular cheap and brands including Woodbines or Park Drive, while Craven 'A', with its black cat symbol, Senior Service and Gold Leaf occupied the medium-strength section. If a 'real' cigarette was required, Player's Weights were regarded as the heavyweights and were guaranteed to make your eyes water! The tall building with the marble pillars and the clock on the wall is the Wesleyan & General Assurance Company. Until 4 July 1953 this is where the Erdington, Short Heath and Tyburn Road trams terminated, and in front of the row of bus stops and loading barriers, the remnants of the tram tracks are still visible. (BC Ref. Lib.)

Opposite below: Having turned left from Snow Hill into Steelhouse Lane, 1239 (FOF 239) is working on the CITY service, the rather anonymous shortworking of the cross-city 29 route, in 1949. It is passing the decoratively fronted, late Victorian Wesleyan General building, which would survive until 1988. Always allocated to Perry Barr garage, this Daimler COG5 was the only one ever to be built with a Brush body. It entered service on 2 December 1939 as one of three bodies speculatively ordered by BCT in their quest for another body supplier although the Second World War rather put paid to that idea. The Brush body had saloon windows that were radiused at the bottom with squared tops. 1239 is carrying an upside-down radiator slip-board which, on its arrival in High Street, would be turned round to show that the bus would be going to Kingstanding. The tram is 642, one of the unique batch of twenty-five MRCW-bodied bogie cars delivered in 1923, which were the first Birmingham trams to be totally enclosed. (J. Whybrow)

Above: Passing between the old Wesleyan General Building and Snow Hill Station on its way northbound out of the city centre is one of the last single-door Daimler Fleetlines to enter service with Birmingham City Transport. 3775 (KOX 775F) was one of fifty Park Royal-bodied buses and this one entered service on 13 March 1968. It is operating the 90 service later the same year. The later Park Royal-bodied Fleetlines had the by-now standard large 'V'-shaped windscreen but this was coupled to a smaller version for the front upper saloon windows. First seen on a Leyland Atlantean PDR1/1 demonstrator, KTD 551C, the design was reminiscent of the last bodies produced by Christopher Dodson of Willesden in 1932 for London 'Pirate' operators. (D. R. Harvey)

Opposite above: During a period when Colmore Circus was being constructed in 1965 and 1966, outbound buses were diverted to run down Livery Street in order to reach Great Hampton Street. Routes affected by this included the 90 route. Travelling out of the city on the 90 route is 2134 (JOJ 134), a Leyland Titan PD2/1 with a Leyland body. It is about to be overtaken by 1732 (HOV 732), which is also on a diversion when working on a 5 route to Court Lane, Perry Common. Both these Leylands were fitted with synchromesh gearboxes, which was standard for the PD2 model. These gearboxes had crash on first gear while the other three were synchromesh, though the gear change from first to second was very slow, so that on the flat most drivers pulled away in the second ratio, usually with some transmission judder. (D. R. Harvey Collection)

Opposite below: The first of the fifty Leyland-bodied Leyland Titan PD2/1s dating from 1949 was 2131 (JOJ 131). Here it is negotiating Colmore Circus in around 1966 when on a 29 route shortworking to Perry Barr whence it will return to its garage at Hockley. These buses, with their powerful Leyland o.600 9.8-litre engines, weighed only 7 tons 10 cwt 3 qtrs, had a good power-to-weight ratio and as a result had a splendid turn of speed, which was ideal for the 74 route to Dudley and the 75 to Wednesbury where there were long stretches between stops. To a lesser extent this was true on the 29 group of services where north of Perry Barr and south of Sparkhill there were parts of the route that were ideally suited to fast running. (J. Carroll)

Picking up a passenger in Snow Hill Ringway in 1965 is 1555 (GOE 555). The bus is opposite Lloyd House and is working on the 90 route back to Kingstanding and the Pheasey Estate. Numerically, 1555 was the last of the seventy-five Daimler CVA6s and entered service on 1 November 1947 and subsequently became one of the last to be withdrawn at the end of July 1966. The Birmingham CVA6s had special engine mountings and did not suffer from the same level of engine vibration found with other operators' examples; this resulted in a comfortable if somewhat stately ride on account of their small engine size. (C. W. Routh)

Lancaster Place–Dale End
29, 29A, 33, 34 90 and 91 routes

The High Street bound 29 and 29A bus routes went from Snow Hill and into Steelhouse Lane passing the old terminus of the Erdington group of tram routes outside the Gaumont Cinema, then down the hill to the General Hospital at the junction with Lower Loveday Street. The buses then went into the large tragfic complex in Lancaster Palace. The area was dominated by the Central Fire Station in front of which numerous bus services crossed with the inbound 29 services turning into Corporation Street but where the inbound 33 route coming into the city from Newtown Row went into Stafford Street before passing through a mixed area of factories and late Victorian houses. On reaching Coleshill Street, used by the 56 bus service to Washwood Heath arrived from its outer suburb, before arriving in the city centre in Dale End. Here the 33 route turned right into Martineau Street where it picked up passengers for its return journey to Kingstanding. THis part of the city centre was redeveloped in the early 1960s when the 75 year leases on the late Victorian properties expired.

Turning across Corporation Place and across the junction with Stafford Street is 2361 (JOJ 361). This exposed-radiator Crossley DD42/6 with a Crossley H30/24R body will turn into Corporation Street before making the long climb past the Victoria Law Courts to the junction with Bull Street when working on a southbound 29A route. Behind the bus is the Central Fire Station, whose foundation stone was laid in March 1934. This block replaced a warren of tightly packed slum properties. The building was finished by December 1935 at a cost of £157,000 and officially opened by the Duke of Kent. (R. H. G. Simpson)

Above: During the construction of James Watt Queensway, several temporary roads were built in order that traffic could continue into the city. Dale End Approach was one such road and replaced Stafford Street as a one-way route towards High Street. The demolition of the properties on the western side of Stafford Street revealed the sheer size of the three-storey Methodist Central Hall built in 1903, whose main entrance is in Corporation Street. Having been latterly one of Highgate Road garage's twenty-seven Crossley-bodied Daimler CVG6s until that garage's closure on 14 July 1962, 2879 (JOJ 879), by now allocated to Yardley Wood garage, passes the temporary concrete shops when it is working on the 29A route during 1964. (T. J. Edgington)

Opposite above: Having left the distant Corporation Place, whereas the 29s took the second exit into Corporation Street, the 33 route took the first exit into Stafford Street on its way to Dale End and Martineau Street. The demolition of the west side of Stafford Street had been completed, while the factories on the right, containing a large furniture manufacturer, would survive for a few more years. By 19 November 1966 when the two-year-old 3396 (396 KOV), a Metro-Cammell-bodied Daimler Fleetline CRG6LX, was negotiating the roadworks and the waste ground. These demolition sites were usually used as temporary car parks and on this Stafford Street site the parked cars include a Standard Ensign, a Vauxhall Victor FB, a Wolseley 1500 and a Ford Zephyr 4 Mk lll saloon. (R. H. G. Simpson)

Opposite below: After the southbound 29A became the 91 route after 29 November 1964, all the services temporarily used the Stafford Street line-of-route variation until the Inner Ring Road scheme had been completed. 2729 (JOJ 729), one of Hockley garage's Metro-Cammell-bodied Daimler CVD6s, passes over a section of temporary road on 5 May 1965. This diverted the road away from the original line of Stafford Street, where the soon-to-be-demolished premises of the electrical tool retailer WH Price stood on the corner of Ryder Street. Following the bus is a Vauxhall Victor F series II. Within four years it would be difficult to identify this location, which was buried underneath Masshouse Ringway, which itself was replaced in the first decade of the twenty-first century. (R. H. G. Simpson)

Above: Martineau Street was the pick-up point of the 33 bus route as well as several other bus services. Martineau Street had the distinction of being the nearest tram terminus to the city centre and this was where the 6 tram route to Perry Barr began its outbound journey. The last trams to operate from Martineau Street were the routes to Alum Rock and Washwood Heath on 1 October 1950. On Saturday 15 October 1960, 1713 (HOV 713), a Brush-bodied Leyland Titan PD2/1, stands at the 33 stop barriers. It will pull away and turn right into Corporation Street. This will be the last time that they will be able to do so in this city-centre street as this is the final day that Martineau Street will be open. Not only will the buses go but so will the street itself, with the expiry of the seventy-five-year leases on the properties. (B. W. Ware)

Opposite above: On the distant corner of Stafford Street and Coleshill Street, which was the original 1923 route of the A47 national route between Birmingham and Great Yarmouth, was the Shah Jahar Indian restaurant. This was one of the earliest Indian restaurants in post-war Birmingham. 1678 (HOV 678), a Leyland Titan PD2/1 with an attractive Brush H30/24R body, has just turned into Dale End when operating on the cross-city 29 route to Highfield Road, Hall Green. Behind it is another of the same type of bus travelling into the city centre on the 33 service. Turning out of Coleshill Street on the 43 route from Nechells is the last of the ten pre-production 1962 Daimler Fleetline CRG6LXs, 3250 (250 DOC). (R. H. G. Simpson)

Opposite below: Dale End became the main A47 route out of the city towards Coleshill and Leicester under the national road-numbering scheme, and its width reflected that it was here, around the fifteenth-century Welch Gate and Market Cross, that Welsh cattle drovers held their cattle market. The whole area was redeveloped in the late Victorian period and behind the Morris Minor car the nineteenth-century building with the clock over it is Hedges the Chemist. The bus is 2106 (JOJ 106), a Daimler CVD6 with a Metro-Cammell H30/24R body dating from June 1951. It is dropping off the last of its passengers near to the junction with Albert Street and it will move off empty before crossing into High Street and turning right into Martineau Street where it will terminate. (J. C. Walker)

On 16 October 1960, the city termini of the 33, 39, 42, 52 and 56 routes were diverted from Martineau Street into the nearby Union Street. One of the trial batch of ten Daimler Fleetline CRG6LXs, 3247 (247 DOC), pulls up the hill in Union Street when leaving for Kingstanding on the 33 route and is indicating that it is about to turn into Corporation Street. It is passing the closed and gated entrance to the City Arcade, which despite appearances was eventually restored to its former glory. Harper Brothers of Heath Hayes began operating a limited-stop service from Brownhills and Cannock into Union Street via Kingstanding on 21 June 1965 and one of their former St Helens Corporation Park Royal-bodied RTs passes Henry's department store, following 3247 out of Union Street. (R. W. Tennent)

Corporation Street (inbound)–Lower Bull Street
25, 29, 29A, 33, 90, 91 and 92 routes

These inbound bus routes left Lancaster place and climbed up the hill in Corporation Street. This was the last section of Joseph Chamberlain's grand Improvement Scheme for the then town centre and for the last few years of the nineteenth century, the only building of note was the large French-styled, red-brick and terracotta Victoria Law Courts which were opened in 1891. Opposite is the Methodist Central Hall built in 1903 with a huge single tower rising above the shops beneath. On reaching Old Square, the site of the last Georgian square in central Birmingham was reached. A number of bus services began from Old Square succeeding the wartime abandoned number 7 trolleybus and had previously been the terminus of a number of late Victorian steam tram services. Since 1929 the section of Corporation Street from Old Square to Lower Bull Street was dominated by the multi-storey Lewis's Department Store. The routes then turned left down Lower Bull Street, which prior to its redevelopment in the 1960s was not wide enough for any bus stops resulting in the services crossing Dale End and stopping in High Street outside the News Theatre and the Oxford Restaurant.

The tall tower at the northern end of Corporation Street belongs to the Methodist Central Hall, constructed in 1903. This section of Chamberlain's 'Parisian boulevard' had only been developed at the turn of the century due to a general downturn in the national economy, which had rather left his 'grand scheme' to peter out before reaching its intended northern destination at Aston Road. The unique Brush-bodied Daimler COG5 1239 (FOF 239) has just left Corporation Place and is travelling up Corporation Street when working on the 29A route. Travelling in the opposite direction is four-wheeler tram 371, which is going on a football special to Villa Park. (J. S. Webb)

Above: Approaching Old Square in Corporation Street on the CITY service is another of Perry Barr garage's Brush-bodied Leyland Titan PD2/1s. With the Methodist Central Hall's tower dominating the skyline of Corporation Street on the right, 1754 (HOV 754), the penultimate Leyland Titan PD2/1 bodied by Brush, travels towards its shortworking terminus in High Street. This 1948-vintage bus is displaying the destination CITY, meaning that it is working on a 29 route from Kingstanding Circle in around 1963. On the right, the Bell, Nicolson & Lunt building is beginning to emerge from behind its construction scaffolding. (R. H. G. Simpson)

Opposite above: Travelling along Corporation Street on an inbound 29 service in 1961 is one of Hockley garage's Crossley-bodied Daimler CVG6s. 3161 (MOF 161) has just passed James Watt Street with the Light of Asia Indian restaurant on the far corner and is passing the marble-fronted shops in the block occupied by the *Birmingham Gazette*, *Evening Despatch* and *Sports Argus* newspapers. Following the bus is an Austin Mini Seven dating from July 1960, while parked on the right is a Morris Minor Series II saloon. (D. R. Harvey Collection)

Opposite below: 'New Look'-fronted MCCW-bodied Daimler CVD6 2103 (JOJ 103) quietly processes along Corporation Street in about 1957 when it still had its original direction trafficator arms. Behind the bus is the former Grand Theatre, which had opened on 14 November 1883 with an auditorium that seated 2,200. Acquired by Moss Empires in 1907, it was closed on 1 September 1930, reopening as a cinema showing the classic Lewis Milestone film *All Quiet on The Western Front* starring Lew Ayres. Alas, after just three years the Grand shut down on 13 May 1933, and after being empty for a few years it reopened in its third incarnation as Mecca Dancing's Grand Casino Ballroom, surviving until 1960 when the whole block was demolished as part of the Priory Queensway redevelopment scheme. Parked outside Blake's Medical Stores on this sunny day in the summer of 1959 is an Austin Sixteen and a Vauxhall HIX Twelve-Four, both dating from around 1947. (S. N. J. White)

Above: The huge Bell, Nicolson & Lunt's wholesale drapery office headquarters dominated the northern side of Old Square and the first section of Corporation Street. The block had been occupied for a few years by the time 3132 (MOF 132) came swinging around the island over the subways of Old Square and into Corporation Street in 1968. This Daimler CVG6 with a Crossley H30/25R body, delivered for service on 1 July 1953, is working on the 90 route back to the Pheasey Estate having operated on just the northern half of the cross-city route. When it was new, 3132 had been used as a demonstrator to both Coventry Corporation in December 1953 and to Glasgow Corporation in January 1954. (A. Yates)

Opposite above: On 11 February 1989, MCW Metrobus Mk I DR102/27 2299 (KJW 299W) turns left into Priory Queensway from Corporation Street. Behind the bus is Lewis's seven-storey building, which was completed in a severe classical design in 1929. The store finally closed its doors on 13 July 1991. 2299 is working on the 91 route and has the WEST MIDLANDS TRAVEL fleet name, which was introduced when this new company was created after bus deregulation on 26 October 1986. This was part of an order for 160 Mark I Metrobuses; originally thirty-five of these were intended to be Volvo Ailsas, but after the order had been approved in March 1981 political pressure to support local industry caused the bus order to go completely to Metro-Cammell. (D. R. Harvey)

Opposite below: With the large Lewis's department store behind it, 1548 (GOE 548), a Daimler CVA6, descends Lower Priory from the distant Corporation Street. Lower Priory was converted to a temporary dual carriageway, though it was operated in the Continental manner with this down side being on the left. This was so that traffic could turn right into Dale End. To the left of the bus is the first of the concrete abutments whose top level would be the future road surface of the replacement Priory Queensway. The bus is being followed by a Morris Minor 1000 car and a Dodge D300 tractor unit, which shared its Motor Panels LAD cab with both Leyland and Albion chassis. (A. E. Hall)

Travelling towards Bull Street junction, having passed Lewis's store in Corporation Street with Old Square behind it on 20 September 1978, is an early standard design of Daimler Fleetline CRG6LX. 4337 (NOB 337M) had a Park Royal H43/33F body. This bus, dating from November 1973, is on a 91 service which will terminate in Lower Bull Street. The Old Square had yet to be filled-in to recreate the more pedestrian-friendly crossing, thus eliminating the subterranean shops below the road level and the troglodyte access to them. Travelling towards Old Square is a Ford Cortina Mark IV, which was in production between 1976 and 1979. (D. R. Harvey)

Above: Standing in Corporation Street, just short of Lower Bull Street, is 1316 (FOF 316), a Leyland-bodied Leyland Titan TD6c which was one of Hockley garage's allocation of eighteen of these vehicles and is operating a cross-city 29 service to Highfield Road, Hall Green, on 3 June 1950. This bus was used in the official publicity photographs by Leyland Motors prior to entering service on 1 November 1939. Possibly the best looking of BCT's pre-war buses, the bodies had many Birmingham fixtures and fittings including a straight staircase. On Saturday 3 June 1950 it is standing at the stops in Corporation Street between Lower Priory and Bull Street. Behind, overhanging the pavement, is the decorative canopy for the Stork Hotel with an Austin Goodwood 14/6 six-cylinder saloon parked outside. Although this section of Corporation Street was one-way towards Bull Street from the distant Old Square, the trams going to Washwood Heath, Alum Rock and Perry Barr from the Martineau Street terminus went against the flow of the motor traffic. Passing Lewis's department store working on the 5 route is 1626 (GOE 626), a Daimler CVG6 with an MCCW H30/24R body that entered service in February 1948. (G. F. Douglas courtesy A. D. Packer)

Opposite above: 'Steaming up' Corporation Street and passing the entrance to Old Square and its subterranean public lavatories in the square's central island is 2186 (JOJ 186). This is one of Hockley garage's small allocation of Park Royal-bodied Leyland Titan PD2/1s dating from 1950 and is working on the 29 route to Highfield Road. It was strange in retrospect that all 201 post-war BCT PD2/1s had non-standard bodywork compared to the undertaking's normal requirements. Whereas the Brush-bodied ones were built with the Loughborough-based coachbuilder's fairly loose, if very handsome, interpretation of BCT's specification and the fifty-one Leyland-bodied buses were effectively bought 'off-the-shelf', the Park Royal ones, numbered 2181–2230, had very little Birmingham 'style' about them although these bodies were at the top end of Park Royal's production, quality being reflected in some of them lasting for nineteen years in service. (W. J. Haynes)

Turning into Lower Bull Street when operating the 29A service on 9 August 1962 is 1550 (GOE 550). Dwarfed by Lewis's department store, this Metro-Cammell-bodied Daimler CVA6 passes the closed-down premises of Dunne's gentleman's outfitters and a blue-painted police phone box. The Daimler CVA6 model was a throwback to the wartime AEC-engined CWA6 model. After the reintroduction of the post-war 'Victory' model by Daimler, the AEC 7.58 litre remained available to the Coventry-based company until 1949 when the supply of these engines was terminated. The CVA6 therefore had a limited following. Coventry Corporation, following on from their unique pre-war COA6 model, received ninety-six of the type, which was the largest number supplied to a UK operator. Birmingham's seventy-five CVA6s were the second-largest number delivered, though uniquely they had flexible engine mountings that made for much smoother than normal idling. The next-largest number was forty for Belfast Corporation, which had Harkness bodies built on Park Royal frames. (D. F. Potter)

Opposite above: After 28 February 1971, a new 92 bus route was instigated which was just a renumbering of the 37 service. This went to the city boundary with Shirley in Hall Green via Stratford Road and was the extension of the 91 service shorts that had previously started in Kingstanding but had terminated in the city centre. This left the 91 to soldier on southbound to Baldwins Lane, the old 29A terminus, while anything going north from either Baldwins Lane or Stratford Road showed 90. 2943 (JOJ 943), a Guy Arab IV, waits to leave the stance in Lower Bull Street in around 1972. This bus was one of a large number of former Birmingham Standards to be equipped with a second offside fog lamp when it appeared that legislation was going to make this compulsory. (D. R. Harvey Collection)

After 6 April 1975, the route numbering was restructured again and the poor passenger had to relearn the route-numbering system. This time the old 90 route became unidirectional once more. 4580 (GOG 580N), the first of fifty Gardner-engined, Park Royal-bodied Daimler Fleetlines dating from June 1975, is doing quite poor business as it waits with apparently only one boarding passenger in Lower Bull Street during September 1981. (D. R. Harvey)

Turning into Dale End from Lower Bull Street next to the Corporation Square Shopping Precinct is 4483 (BJ03 EWR), a Wright-bodied Volvo B7TL. On 4 November 2003, when the bus was around six months old, it is seen working on the Line 33 from here in the city centre back to Pheasey via Kingstanding. This was the then terminus of the 33 route, which was actually further away from the city centre than fifty-three years earlier, when it terminated in the long-lost Martineau Street. (D. R. Harvey)

High Street–New Street
25, 29, 29A, 34, 90, 91, 92, 98 and 998 routes

With the exception of the 33 route which started in Martineau Street but after Saturday 15 October 1960, left the city centre from the adjacent Union Street, all the other Kingstanding bus routes used the route through the heart of Birmingham leaving from either outside the Co-operative department store in High Street or just around the corner in front of the Odeon Cinema in High Street. Buses leaving to go to the southern suburbs on the 29 group of routes caried straight on from High Street and turned into the Bull Ring. Both High Street and New Street were part of the sixteenth century part of Birmingham and by the last years of Queen Elizabeth's reign were both lined by stalls and traders. Both streets were substantially developed as important shopping streets in the latter half of the Victorian period, in response to the opening of New Street Railway Station in 1852, but during the Second World War both were extensively damaged in severe air raids leading in part to the dramatic redevelopment of Birmingham's City Centre in the 1950s and 1960s.

With the remnants of Dale End visible just to the right of the bus and the original junction into Albert Street being marked by the Ford Escort turning into it, 2847 (JOJ 847) has come down Lower Bull Street when working on the 90 service back to Kingstanding Circle. 2847 (JOJ 847) was the most distinctive of all Birmingham's Standard buses built between 1950 and 1954, having been involved in an accident and sent to Midland Red's Carlyle Road works, where the rear area was completely restyled with an enclosed platform and electrically operated doors. The bus also received a Cave-Brown-Cave heating system and yellow-painted ceilings before re-entering service on 10 December 1959. This conversion added almost 3 cwt and looked very neat from the rear, but the frame did not match up with the nearside distinctive curvature of the body, so had a somewhat ungainly look from certain angles. From the front, the only clue to this major rebuilding was the ventilator grill over the half-cab canopy. (D. R. Harvey Collection)

Above: Waiting at the 29 and 29A bus stop outside the Oxford Restaurant and Snack Bar, which sold the most lovely steak and kidney pies and Cornish pasties, in High Street between Albert Street and Carrs Lane in High Street, is Park Royal-bodied Leyland Titan PD2/1 2195 (JOJ 195). Although bought because the London-based coachbuilder could meet an urgent delivery date, they were of a non-standard body design although they were equipped with BCT's fixtures and fittings; the resultant vehicles were extremely handsome. The design was spoilt only by the almost wartime opening window at the front of the lower saloon in lieu of opening bulkhead hoppers. 2195 is working on the 29 route to Highfield Road. (Midland OPS)

Opposite above: By Sunday 2 April 1989, the Corporation Square shopping area on the corner of Lower Bull Street and Dale End had been completed. Preserved 2489 (JOJ 489), a 1950-vintage 'New Look' concealed-front Crossley DD42/6 with a Crossley H30/24R body, stands in High Street and is displaying the cross-city 34 destination. It will cross the city centre by way of New Street and Stephenson Street before going to Quinton by way of Holloway Head and Hagley Road. (D. R. Harvey)

Opposite below: In around 1967, 3389 (389 KOV) stands in High Street as it waits for passengers when being employed on the 90 service. This was the penultimate 'flat-fronted' Metro-Cammell-bodied seventy-two-seater Daimler Fleetline CRG6LX and had entered service on 2 August 1964, lasting with WMPTE until April 1979. It is being overtaken by Miller Street garage's 3137 (MOF 137), a Daimler CVG6 which is proceeding to the Union Street terminus of the Beeches Estate 52 route. (D. R. Harvey Collection)

The graceful lines of the Brush body on Leyland Titan PD2/1 1681 (HOV 681) are clearly shown as it stands in High Street after a heavy shower of rain. It is on the 91 service and has the small black waistrail fleet numbers that were introduced in 1962. These were among the first Leyland Titan PD2s to be built and although they were PD2/1s, the chassis had modifications to BCT specifications, thus the official PD2 Special designation. Their bodies were the first production post-war metal-framed manufactured by Brush, and were based on the 1946 prototype built for BCT and fitted to Daimler COG5 1235 (FOF 235). The body quality was excellent and they were fitted with the BCT straight staircase as well as being the first buses to be delivered with a twin-skinned upper deck ceiling. Unfortunately a series of mistakes was made with regard to the demanding Birmingham specification, not least that the first 80 of the 100 bodies had their patterned moquette put on sideways! They were long-lasting bodies but they were also the last bodies built for BCT by Brush. (D. R. Harvey Collection)

The rebuilding of the Dale End and Lower Priory areas to the north-east of the main central shopping area had enormous ramifications elsewhere. The road was closed due to repair works in Lower Bull Street as Daimler CVA6 1540 (GOE 540), when being used on the 90 route back to the Pheasey Estate in around 1965, travels across the tarred-over tram tracks at the junction with Carrs Lane. The lower part of Bull Street was always a narrow, thriving thoroughfare which never really looked like the rest of Birmingham's Victorian shopping area. The semi-circular building on the corner of Bull Street and Dale End had been originally owned from the 1880s by Reece Brothers, whose shop sign had declared it to be 'Ye Oldyst Tobaconyst Shop in Bermyngham'. Preedy's tobacconist's shop lay behind the pedestrian barriers, which followed the curvature of the corner into Dale End. The whole of this area was demolished at the end of the 1960s. Next door in the same three-storey block is one of Birmingham's first Thornton's Chocolate Kabins; this was one of the Sheffield confectioner's first forays into the West Midlands and coincidentally was just a stone's throw from where John Cadbury's first chocolate factory was established in 1824. (D. R. Harvey Collection)

Above: The conductor leans against the headlight of re-bodied Daimler COG5 978 (COX 978) as the bus is parked outside the Co-operative store in High Street in around 1953. It is being employed on the 29 service. 978 entered service on 1 May 1937 with a Metro-Cammell body, but in March 1949 it received the English Electric H28/24R body designed for Manchester Corporation which had formerly been fitted to similar bus 842. The curved window lines of these bodies were the remnants of the Art Deco-style livery employed in Manchester, but the more sober Birmingham livery did reflect the body curves by the upper blue band following these swooping window pans. (BC Ref. Lib.)

Opposite above: Travelling down the hill in Carrs Lane from High Street, where just over twenty years earlier the last Corporation trams had coasted into Moor Street on their way for scrapping, 3141 (MOF 141) works on a 91 service to Baldwins Lane in around 1972. It is overtaking 3754 (KOX 754F), a Park Royal-bodied Daimler Fleetline CRG6LX which is loading up before working on a 53E shortworking to Bordesley Green. In the distance is one of Harper Brothers' Northern Counties-bodied Daimler Fleetlines. (A. Yates)

Opposite below: It might seem surprising that during the height of Second World War life went on as normal, but here is evidence! Pedestrians, shoppers, children and military personnel walk along the bomb-damaged High Street in 1944, which was badly bombed in an air raid on the night of 9 April 1941, when all the buildings on the extreme left into New Street were destroyed. Later this huge area of derelict land became known as the 'Big Top' site after a series of large marquees were erected there. Behind the bus are the remnants of High Street's eastern-side shops that had survived the bombing. The gap behind the bus is where Marks & Spencer's Bazaar was located, while the modern square block on the corner of Carrs Lane is the late 1930s premises of Jay's furniture store. The driver of 1021 (CVP 121) walks in front of his bus before getting into his cab and driving off to Yardley Wood railway station in Highfield Road on the 29 service. Approaching High Street from Dale End is a 1937 Standard Flying Fourteen fitted with small wartime headlights. Parked outside Slater's & Bodega's wine merchant, this Metro-Cammell-bodied Daimler COG5 managed to operate a full fourteen-year life without undergoing a body swap. (BC Ref. Lib.)

Above: After the buildings on the corner of New Street and the Bull Ring were demolished, but before the Rotunda Building was started, 2363 (JOJ 363) stands in front of the Lloyds Bank building, built in 1875, which was on the corner of Worcester Street. 2363, a Crossley-bodied exposed-radiator Crossley DD42/6 dating from 1 February 1950, is well loaded-up when about to leave the bus stop when working on the 29 route to Kings Road, Kingstanding, having worked across the southern suburbs from Highfield Road, Hall Green. (PhotoFives)

Opposite above: The long-drawn-out process of getting the 'New Look'-front Daimler CVD6s bodied by Metro-Cammell limped along very slowly. The last of the exposed-radiator examples, ending with 2030, had entered service on New Year's Day 1950, but the first of these attractive-looking buses, beginning with 2031, did not take to the road until mid-September 1950. It took until August 1951 for the order for 100 buses to be completed. The reason for this delay was because Metro-Cammell prioritised the lucrative body orders for London Transport as well as their own standard designs. Specialist designs, such as those for Birmingham, had to wait until materials and opportunities became available. 2087 (JOJ 87), dating from March 1951, is still in its first year of service as it stands outside the Co-operative department store in High Street. It was here that the crews took their timing break, which is why the driver is not in his cab. 2087, like all the Daimler-engined Daimlers, did not have a long life and was withdrawn on 30 September 1966. (D. R. Harvey Collection)

Opposite below: The express service to the Circle at Kingstanding was introduced as the 98 service on 1 April 1968. It started outside the Odeon cinema in New Street and left the city by way of Snow Hill and Summer Lane. The Odeon opened as the Paramount on 4 September 1937 with the film *The Charge of the Light Brigade* and had an exceptionally fine four-manual Compton cinema organ. During October 1977, the express bus route was renumbered 998, but by that time it had been extended to Pheasey Estate. Former BCT Daimler Fleetline CRG6LX 3607 (FOC 607D) pulls into New Street beneath the Rotunda Building. Hidden behind the bus is the short remnant of the old Bull Ring that led to the Inner Ring Road at St Martin's Circus. (D. R. Harvey Collection)

Above: Speeding along New Street and going towards the junction with Corporation Street is 2136 (JOJ 136), a 1949-vintage Leyland-bodied Leyland Titan PD2/1. It is running on the 29A bus service in August 1963 with the Arden Hotel towering over New Street. Loading up with passengers in front of Littlewood's store is a BMMO D7 with a Metro-Cammell body. 4403 (VHA 403) is operating on the 168 route to Coleshill. In the distance is High Street, with the Art Deco-style eight-storey Times Furnishing building completed in 1938. (D. R. Harvey Collection)

Opposite above: In late 1968, 2485 (JOJ 485), a 'New Look'-front Crossley DD42/6 is working on the shortworking numbered 90F to Perry Barr. The use of the suffix letters had been introduced in 1953 but it was only by 1968 that these had been universally applied to all the destination shortworkings. It is pulling out from behind the Norfolk Hotel's courtesy Austin Mini Traveller Estate car as it leaves the bus stop. Overtaking the Crossley is Midland Red's 6023 (LHA 623F), a Daimler Fleetline CRG6LX with an Alexander body, which in May 1968 had been converted to a two-door H43/28D layout as a prototype for the next batch of the company's double-deckers. Towering above New Street is the iconic, cylindrical Rotunda building in whose podium was the new Lloyds Banking Hall, which had replaced the building next to 2485. (D. R. Harvey Collection)

Opposite below: Looking towards the junction with Corporation Street and the distant columns of the Town Hall in Victoria Square, 2546 (JOJ 546), a 1950 former BCT Metro-Cammell-bodied Guy Arab III Sp, stands outside the Odeon Cinema in 1975. It is loading up with passengers when working on a 90 service, while beyond are the long rows of bus shelters showing just how important New Street was as a terminal point for the city's bus services. Dominating New Street is King Edward House, which was completed in 1938 and for many years had housed Littlewood's store. (D. R. Harvey Collection)

The Gothic-style premises on the corner of Stephenson Place and New Street was the magnificently pinnacled Exchange Building. It had been built for the trading of coal and other merchandise. This building was opened on 2 January 1865 and was then the largest and most impressive commercial building in Birmingham, containing offices, meeting rooms and dining, drinking and smoking facilities. In November 1879 it was equipped with the town's first telephone exchange with initially fewer than a dozen subscribers. The Exchange Building was cruelly demolished in 1965 when the rebuilding of New Street station began. Ten years earlier on 4 May 1955, Daimler CVA6 1484 (GOE 484), the fourth post-war Birmingham bus to be delivered, is dwarfed by the Exchange Building as it prepares to turn right into Corporation Street when operating on the 29A route. (BC Ref. Lib.)

Corporation Street, Bull Street and Victoria Square
25, 29, 29A, 33, 90, 91, 92, 98 and 998 routes

The City Centre one-way street system introduced in 1933 was something of a music hall joke and provided visiting motorists with what appeared to be a maze of right angled turns, no entry signs and the feeling that once into it one wouldn't get out. Yet this was where the northbound group of bus services travelled seemingly without difficulty. Corporation Street was created in the late 1870s and was lined with impressive large shops with offices above mainly in the French Renaissance style. Buses met the inbound services at Bull Street but turned left into this much older street to arrive at Snow Hill. The peak hour 25 route, on its inbound journey, on reaching Snow Hill turned right into Colmore Row, redeveloped after 1866 from an important Georgian residential area and becoming a prosperous business and baking area passing the Queen Anne-styled St Phillip's Cathedral and churchyard. It terminated just beyond Waterloo Street opposite Birmingham's huge Council House built over a five year period from 1874 to the designs of the delightfully named Yeoville Thomason.

1681 (HOV 681), built in 1948, turns from New Street into Corporation Street when operating on the 90 route in 1965, not long after the route had been renumbered on 29 November 1964. The rear view of the Brush metal-framed body on this Leyland Titan PD2/1 reveals just how different these bodies were from the standard Birmingham specification. The Brush body was based on the post-war prototype body built in 1946 and placed on pre-war Daimler COG5 1235 (FOF 235). From the rear they resembled pre-war Metro-Cammell bodies with their twin rear upper-saloon emergency windows. (D. R. Harvey Collection)

Above: The Birmingham Shopping Centre was opened in 1971 as part of the reconstruction of Birmingham New Street railway station. Although later renamed The Pallasades, it has never been a successful enterprise, as access from New Street, behind the parked cars on the left, is by a long, awkward ramp. Leyland-engined Leyland Fleetline 6303 (KON 303P), bodied by Metro-Cammell and dating from January 1976, comes up the hill in Corporation Street. It is used on the 92 route, which had been extended from the Hall Green boundary at the old tram and 37 bus terminus through Shirley to the junction with Cranmore Boulevard, Monkspath, in early April 1975. (D. R. Harvey Collection)

Opposite above: Making the same manoeuvre into Corporation Street as 1681 is Daimler CVD6 2025 (JOJ 25). This Metro-Cammell H30/24R-bodied bus entered service in January 1950 and is working on the 29 route to Kingstanding Road. Behind the bus in New Street on the corner of Stephenson Place is the Gothic-style Exchange Building whose ground floor was dominated by Barclays Bank, beyond the traffic lights; next door to the bank is the premises of Polyphoto, who specialised in portrait photography. One of Perry Barr garage's exposed-radiator Daimler CVD6s makes a comparatively rare foray onto the 29A route. 2025 (JOJ 25), one of the attractive-looking fifty-four seaters with MCCW bodywork, passes into Corporation Street from New Street. (A. J. Douglas)

Opposite below: By June 1966, the Victorian Exchange Building had been demolished and a new construction was being erected by the Taylor Woodrow Group. In the distance at the bottom of Stephenson Place is the soon-to-be-knocked-down frontage of New Street station and the adjacent Queens Hotel. Turning from the western end of New Street into Corporation Street is 3081 (MOF 81), one of Quinton garage's allocation of thirty-three Metro-Cammell-bodied Guy Arab IVs. It is operating on the cross-city northbound 33 route from Quinton to Kingstanding, while when going south the bus showed 34. (F. W. York)

Above: At the time of writing, today's Corporation Street has been pedestrianised while the extension of the Midland Metro tram route is being completed. In the 1960s everyday traffic used the one-way street going across the central area of the city. 2183 (JOJ 183), a Park Royal-bodied Leyland Titan PD2/1, is caught in traffic as it crosses the junction with Cherry Street in 1966 when working on the 90 route. Alongside the bus is a Vauxhall Victor FB while between the Corporation bus and the Midland Red BMMO D9 double-decker are a Morris Minor and a 1956 Rover 75 car. (D. R. Harvey Collection)

Opposite above: After the limited-stop 98 service was introduced on 1 April 1968, Perry Barr garage's bus of choice was one of their Strachan-bodied Ford R192s. BCT still had twenty-four 1950 Leyland Tiger PS2/1s on their strength, and when there was a shortage of the Fords these elderly single-deckers were pressed into service. The attractive thirty-four-seat Weymann-bodied single-deckers were fast and reliable despite their age, and twelve of them were converted to OMO in 1967. 2247 (JOJ 247) was one of the last to be returned to service after this conversion and is seen working on an evening 98 service in Corporation Street in 1968. Both the Fords and the Leylands had synchromesh gearboxes, but even at this late stage there was no contest for a 'real' bus driver when the Ford's 5.42-litre engines were compared to the 9.8-litre ones fitted to the PS2/1s. (D. R. Harvey Collection)

Opposite below: The bus passing the bus stops beneath the large clock over H. Samuel's jewellery shop in Corporation Street is being somewhat underused as it works on the 25 service to Finchley Road. The bus is between Fore Street and Cherry Street, but has apparently no passengers on board. 1509 (GOE 509), a Daimler CVA6 with a Metro-Cammell H30/24R body, entered service on 15 August 1947 and by 1962, its penultimate year of service, was allocated to Birchfield Road garage. (J. C. Walker)

Travelling down Corporation Street before the one-way system was introduced in 1933, one of BCT's last outside-staircase buses works its way through the milling pedestrians as it moves towards the New Street junction. 324 (VP 1188), an ADC 507 with a fifty-seat Short Brothers body, is working on the 29 route. The bus entered service in January 1929 but despite it being top covered and having an enclosed cab, these buses could not compete with the AEC Regents delivered later in the same year. As a result they soon looked old-fashioned and became obsolete. As a result, 324 was withdrawn by June 1937. A similar bus, 329 (VP 1193), follows the 29 bus when working on the 15A route. (D. R. Harvey Collection)

In February 1991, West Midlands Travel 2693 (A693 UOE), a Mark II MCW Metrobus, speeds along Corporation Street when operating on the limited-stop 998 service to Kingstanding. It has already passed Rackham's department store, which had opened in November 1960, and is about to turn left into Bull Street. This Metrobus, which had entered service in November 1983, was unusual because of the position of its front number plate. (D. R. Harvey)

CORPORATION STREET, BIRMINGHAM. 36

Above: Loading up with passengers outside Greys department store in Bull Street on what seems to be a 'three bell load' is bus 446 (OV 4446) on the 25 route. This is a petrol-engined AEC Regent 661 whose chassis was built in 1931. This bus was re-bodied in September 1943 with a Brush MoS 'utility' H30/21R body, which as well as retaining the seats and the fixtures and fittings from its original Short Brothers body also included the BCT straight staircase. 446 still had its upper-saloon emergency windows unglazed and the rear dome and roof are still painted in the camouflaged grey livery. (D. R. Harvey Collection)

Opposite: Turning into Bull Street from Corporation Street in around 1934 is bus 445 (OV 4445). This bus was a 1931-registered AEC Regent 661 with a Short H27/21R body. It is operating on the 29 route to Kingstanding. Towering over it is the recently completed Lewis's department store, which occupied the block from Bull Street to Old Square. This bus was one of thirty which were able to briefly respond to the appeal by London Transport for provincial buses to operate after the first German air raids over the capital. 445 operated from Turnham Green garage from late October to the end of November 1940 but was returned to Birmingham because of a similar shortage of buses due to air raids in the city. Tram 337 travels against the normal traffic flow in Corporation Street as it goes to Witton Square via Six Ways, Newtown, on the 3 route. (Commercial Postcard)

Above: On Sundays, the night-service buses continued until 7.00 a.m. rather than the 5.00 a.m. last departures between Mondays and Saturdays. The services left on the hour all through the night, and the NS29A started in Bull Street. Waiting in July 1962 outside Grey's department store on the last Sunday-morning departure is the eleven-year-old 2111 (JOJ 111), a Daimler CVD6 with an MCCW H30/24R body dating from June 1951. The night service went beyond Kingstanding Circle but only to the Lambeth Road-Queslett Road junction, some 500 yards short of the daytime terminus at Collingwood Drive. (PhotoFives)

Oposite above: Passing the former Grey's department store, which appears to be in the first throws of demolition, in Bull Street in 1993 is 2750 (A750 WVP). The bus is working on the 90 service to Pheasey. This 1984 Mark II MCW Metrobus dating from June 1984 could be easily distinguished from the Mark I, one of which, 2391 (LOA 391X) delivered in December 1981, is to the left and is working on the 79 service to Wolverhampton – it has a large symmetrical windscreen, a fussier looking front grill panel and thicker body pillars. (D. R. Harvey)

Opposite below: Lewis's department store building looms large over 3215 (MOF 215). The bus has turned from Corporation Street into Bull Street when working on the 90 route in around 1968. In the distance is Barrows high-class grocery store, which occupied this site in Lower Bull Street from 1849 until December 1973. This Crossley-bodied Daimler CVG6 has a destination blind taken from a withdrawn exposed-radiator bus, thus showing the number 90 twice. The Corporation bus is being followed by a 36-foot-long Midland Red Leyland Leopard, which is working on the long X12 service to Derby via Lichfield. (A. J. Douglas)

Standing outside Winchester House in Victoria Square is one of the few Morris-Commercial Imperials to survive beyond the end of the Second World War, not being withdrawn until July 1946. 521 (OC 521), which had entered service on 22 September 1933, its wings and mudguards freshly repainted to cover the wartime white edging, is working on the 25 route to Kingstanding in the summer of 1945. Unlike the wings, the roof and rear dome are still painted in camouflage grey. The attractive metal-framed Metro-Cammell bodies on the Imperials were among the first buses to have a modern straight front profile and were reseated to H30/24R two years later. Behind 521 are the offices of the Canadian Pacific Railway Company, who always had a wonderfully large, detailed model of one of their latest ships as their window display. (R. Marshall Collection)

On 13 June 1964, 1709 (HOV 709), a 1948-vintage Leyland Titan PD2/1 with a Brush H30/24R body, pulls away from the bus stop in front of the Blue Star Line shipping company's offices in Victoria Square before turning in front of Galloway's Corner and into New Street. The Blue Star Line was a British passenger and cargo shipping company formed in 1911, who had developed refrigerated ships to import frozen meat from South America to Britain. Unusually for a Birmingham City Transport bus, the destination blind is not set correctly – the bus is going to Finchley Road, Kingstanding, on the 25 service. Behind the Leyland and passing Waterloo Street is 2894 (JOJ 894), a Crossley-bodied Daimler CVG6 which is operating on the 32 service. (R. Moss)

Around the Bull Ring
29, 29A, 30, 34, 90, 91 and 92 routes

This was the start of where the 29 group of bus services left the city centre towards the south half of the routes. This was the traditional heart of Birmingham centred on St Martin's Parish Church. This Victorian building stands on the original site of a pre-Norman chapel which served a population of less than 100 souls. The Bull Rind is on a very steep hill, just above the church and below the junction with High Street. In this area there have been retail markets since the twelfth century. The whole area including the Chales Edge's majestic Doric-porched Market Hall opened on 12 February 1835, was swept away in the early 1960s by the original Bull RIng Shopping Centre and the twenty-five storey circular office block Rotunda all being completed by 29 May 1964 when the huge shopping centre was opened. Alas with subterranean passages and poor access from the City Centre, the Bull Ring area gradually fell into decline and it was only the total second redevelopment, completed in 2003 that finally banished all traffic away from the area, icnluding all the bus services.

Speeding along Moor Street Queensway in around 1970, a former Acocks Green garage Guy Arab IV 6LW, 2971 (JOJ 971), is heading towards The Bull Ring. It is operating on the 34 route to the Hagley Road West terminus in Quinton. By this time 2971 had been transferred to Quinton garage, though its time there was not long as the bus was withdrawn in August 1971. Passing the bus is an Austin Westminster A110 Mk II. (F. W. York)

On 22 March 1980, 7003 (WDA 3T), a thirteen-month-old Leyland Titan TNLXB1RF with a Park Royal H47/26F body, stands in the bus lay-by in Moor Street Queensway. This bus was delivered in this livery, which had a deep cream band below the lower-saloon windows. On the other side of the Queensway is the architectural gem of St Michael's Roman Catholic Church. It was built in 1802 as a Nonconformist chapel for the Unitarian Church in New Meeting Street to replace the building burned down in the so-called Priestley riots of 1791. It is a rectangular building with a pedimented Georgian façade and four sets of paired Ionic pilasters. The Unitarians were an influential Nonconformist Christian church in Birmingham, whose Victorian philanthropic, social and community work, undertaken by influential families such as the Chamberlains, Kenricks, Martineaus and Rylands, became legendary in the town. In the 1860s the chapel became redundant and went from one end of the Christian spectrum to the other, being sold to the Roman Catholic Church, becoming St Michael's. It narrowly escaped the 'let's pull it down if it's old' school of town planning that so decimated Birmingham's city centre in the 1960s. (F. W. York)

Above: Swinging round St Martin's Circus with Smallbrook Ringway's shops in the background is a bus working on the 30 route to Kings Road, Kingstanding. With the car park of the Bull Ring shopping centre on the other side of Manzoni Gardens, 2157 (JOJ 157), a Leyland-bodied Leyland Titan PD2/1, has its left-hand flashing indicator on as it slows down for the stop next to The Rotunda. It will then turn left into New Street to stop outside the Odeon cinema which was virtually on the other side of the Rotunda. (PhotoFives)

Opposite above: On a rainy March day in 1984, a former Leyland-engined Daimler Fleetline 4563 (GOG 563N), dating from March 1975, passes beneath the connecting bridge which linked High Street to the Bull Ring shopping centre. The Park Royal-bodied bus, allocated to Yardley Wood garage, is working on the cross-city 90 route to Pheasey Estate. Behind 4563 are two more WMPTE standard-bodied Fleetlines which have come from the Bull Ring. Overtaking the bus is a Hillman Imp, a very fast and underrated rear-engined mini car. (D. R. Harvey)

Opposite below: 2124 (JOJ 124), a 1951 Daimler CVD6 with an MCCW body, travels towards High Street from the Bull Ring and is about to pass the grassed area of Manzoni Gardens in the middle of St Martin's Circus. The bus is working on the 29 service to Kingstanding Circle in November 1964, not long after the huge Bull Ring Centre had been opened by Prince Philip on 29 May 1964. It had a mixture of traditional open-air market stalls in front of the building and was the first indoor city-centre shopping centre in the UK. The shopping centre had cost an estimated £8 million and covered 23 acres with 140 shops. The gardens had been named after the Birmingham city architect Sir Herbert Manzoni, who had been responsible for the design of the Inner Ring Road but also for the brutal demolition of many fine buildings in the city centre. (D. R. Harvey Collection)

On 27 August 1990, a by-now West Midlands Travel-owned Mark I MCW Metrobus 2285 (KJW 285W), travels along St Martin's Circus beneath the shadow of the Rotunda when working on the 91 route. It has another variation on the destination display of PHEASEY, but with HOCKLEY displayed in the bottom blind box. Behind the bus, built on the roof raft over New Street station, is the Pallasades shopping centre, renamed from the Birmingham shopping centre. On the right, the brick building with the large advertising boarding is the back of the Odeon Cinema which stands on New Street. This section of road, known as St Martins Circus, does not exist as it was removed, although the Manzoni Gardens and the Bull Ring Centre during the redevelopment of the area when the new Bullring was bieng developed. (D. R. Harvey)

The steep slope of the Bull Ring was the heart of Birmingham, standing in front of St Martin's Parish Church. The Bull Ring dated back to the twelfth century as a marketplace and remained a vibrant place until much of it fell victim to the air raids of the Second World War. Loading up with passengers next to what, in Birmingham, was known as 'a bomb building site' is bus 1513 (GOE 513), a Daimler CVA6 with a Metro-Cammell H30/24R body dating from 1 September 1947. It is operating on a southbound 29A service to Baldwins Lane in around 1956. Behind it, being used as a driver training vehicle, is 1937 Daimler COG5 1024 (CVP 124). On the left in the centre of the Bull Ring is the statue of Admiral Lord Nelson, unveiled on 25 October 1809. Although it was one of the smallest memorials erected to the memory of the victor of the battles of Aboukir Bay, Copenhagen and Trafalgar, it had the distinction of being the first in the country, predating Nelson's Column in London by more than thirty years. In front of the statue is the spot unofficially called 'Orators' Corner', where people would talk to anyone who would listen, not just about 'Jesus and Salvation', but about political or social issues of the day. Behind the statue on the other side of Bell Street, and with Doric columns flanking its entrance portico, is Charles Edge's majestic, but by now roofless, Doric-porched Market Hall, which was opened on 12 February 1835 at the then colossal cost of £73,266. The Market Hall was huge, with a capacity of 600 stalls, and measured 365 feet by 106 feet, with an equally impressive entrance in Worcester Street. On the night of 25 August 1940, in one of the first major air raids on the city centre, the Market Hall was reduced to a shell; the almost impregnable outer walls stood for another twenty-two years as an open-air market until it too fell victim in 1962 to the demolisher's ball. On the other side of Phillips Street is the early nineteenth-century Board Inn, which would also disappear in the 1960s redevelopment of the Bull Ring. (BC Ref. Lib.)

Above: About to pull away from the bus stop in the rebuilt Bull Ring on 24 February 1962 is 1716 (HOV 716). This was one of Perry Barr garage's allocation of Brush-bodied Leyland Titan PD2/1s. It is well laden with passengers and its powerful Leyland o.600 9.8-litre engine would make 'mincemeat' of the steep climb outside St Martin's Parish Church as it travels into the city centre. Opposite is St Martin's House multi-storey car park and the early nineteenth-century Royal George M & B-owned public house on the corner of the distant Park Street, which was closed on 3 January 1962 and replaced by a new building. (R. S. A. Redmond)

Opposite above: Oswald Bailey's Army and Navy Stores occupied the late Georgian premises on the corner of the Bull Ring and Moor Street, which had been built as the Temperance Hotel. Having survived the devastating bombing in the area of the Bull Ring, this historic building was swept away as part of the redevelopment of the area in the 1960s. In 1950, bus 2006 (JOJ 6), a brand new Daimler CVD6 with a Metro-Cammell H30/24R body, stands on the cobbles of the Bull Ring when working on a 29 service to Highfield Road. On the radiator is a slip board with lettering VIA SNOW HILL for when the bus was coming into the city from Kingstanding. (R. Hannay)

Opposite below: By the time that the new Bull Ring shopping centre had been completed there was virtually nothing left of the old Bull Ring; even the road layout had changed. The Rotunda was part of the original Bull Ring shopping centre designed by James A. Roberts, and included a twenty-five-storey circular office block and a bank. Construction began on the 271-foot building in 1961 and by the time it had opened in 1965, the Rotunda had cost £1 million and served as a focal point for the area. The new Bull Ring below St Martin's Circus had a curve in it in order to line up with the original roadway south of St Martin's Parish Church and Park Street. Bus 1674 (HOV 674), a Leyland Titan PD2/1 with a Brush body, speeds down the hill and into this chicane when going to Baldwins Lane on a 91 service in 1966. It had passed the multi-storey car park for St Martin's House office block as a Ford Cortina 113E four-door saloon squeezes between the wall of the central reservation and the bus. (R. Beesley)

Climbing from the top of Digbeth into Bull Ring is 2148 (JOJ 148). This Leyland Titan PD2/1 has an H30/26R Leyland body and is running on a northbound 90 service to Pheasey on 24 July 1965. Coming out of St Martin's Lane is a Wolseley 6/80 saloon registered in West Bromwich in 1952; these cars were more usually seen as the archetypal police car. The premises behind the bus date from the 1950s and replaced wartime bombed buildings. After the construction of the new Bullring in 2003 the pub behind the car became known as the Bull Ring Tavern. (Vectis Photographs)

The Southern Half

Digbeth– Camp Hill
5, 29, 29A, 30, 34, 90, 91 and 92 routes

Descending down the sandstone hill from the Bull Ring, the 29 group fo services going to Hall Green arrived in Digbeth, which had been the original location of a Saxon settlement at a crossing point of the River Rea. This was the area in the city where the wholesale fruit, vegetable and meat markets were located as well as many of the types of small factories and workshops that made Birmingham famous as 'the City of a Thousand and One trades'. On reaching Rea Street where the Midland Red bus garage was located, the route crossed the culverted River Rea whereupon the road became High Street, Deritend and later High Street, Bordesley. At Heath Mill Lane, just beyond the Bird's Custard factory was the Od Crown Public House, originally built in 1368 as a mansion house. The next major road junction was at Bordesley Railway Station where Coventry Road, (A45), branched to the left under the railway bridge. Here the temporary Camp Hill Flyover was opened on 15 October 1961 in order to take the southbound carriageway of the A41 over the junction and on to Camp Hill. The flyover lasted for 26 years, before being demolished in 1987. The steep climb passing the large factory of Dowding & Mills took the route up to the 1850s shopping centre at Camp Hill and the famous Ship Inn on the corner of Sandy Lane.

Above: Coming into the city centre in Moat Lane is 4191 (Y796 TOH). This newly repainted Dennis Trident with an Alexander H45/28F body is working on the 5 service on 2 March 2009. The 5 route had its outer terminus at Solihull Station and went via Shirley to the old terminus at Baldwins Lane. This successor to the 29A route then proceeded into the city centre but due to a different road layout it now passes the open-air markets behind Digbeth. (D. R. Harvey)

Opposite above: Passing down Digbeth on the 29 service in 1964 is 2364 (JOJ 364), a Crossley-bodied Crossley DD42/6. These buses were the first double-deckers in the fleet to have sliding saloon ventilators. In the background is the Victorian Gothic-style St Martin's Parish Church in the Bull Ring. It must have been a hot day as the driver has the windscreen of this Crossley-bodied bus open. The cabs of all BCT Crossleys were commodious affairs with easy access for the driver. If there was a problem with these buses, it was that they had manual four-speed gearboxes and heavy steering. This gearbox was one of the first successful synchromesh units and was considerably easier to use than the comparable type fitted to the contemporary BCT Leyland Titan PD2/1s. (R. H. G. Simpson)

Opposite below: Speeding down Digbeth and about to pass the junction with Allison Street is Daimler CVA6 1550 (GOE 550). This Metro-Cammell-bodied bus was working on the 91 route to Baldwins Lane towards the end of its career and is being overtaken by a Ford Zephyr 4 Mk III. Off the picture to the right is Digbeth Police Station, which dated from 1911. On the Allison Street corner is the Midland Red Sports & Social Club and beyond that the Lightfoot Refrigeration factory. At the top of the distant hill is the Bull Ring with St Martin's Parish Church, the Bull Ring shopping centre and the towering Rotunda office block. (D. R. Harvey Collection)

When the 29 route was introduced on 6 February 1928 from Highfield Lane, Hall Green, across the city centre to the Boar's Head on Aldridge Road, it went via Bradford Street, the wholesale markets area, Hurst Street, New Street, Corporation Street, Bull Street and Snow Hill. The later, more straightforward route to the south from the city centre was from High Street via Digbeth and was introduced on 4 November 1934. 127 (OM 226) was one of the first batch of thirty buses delivered with top-covered upper saloons. This AEC 504 had a 6.8-litre petrol engine and was fitted with a Short Brothers fifty-two-seat body with an outside staircase, an open cab and rubber tyres. It had entered service in 6 January 1925 and was converted to operate on pneumatic tyres about three years later. It is parked on a very wet and miserable day in Bradford Street facing Camp Hill when working on the 29 route. 127 is next to the Anchor Inn Public House on the corner of Rea Street with the tarpaulin cab sheeting pulled up to protect the driver from the elements. (O S)

Opposite below: Travelling out of the city centre in Digbeth is a Brush-bodied Leyland Titan PD2/1, which is being used on the 29A route. 1686 (HOV 686) is passing the showrooms of Smithfield Garage, just beyond the junction with Meriden Street. Smithfield Garage was a Rootes Group sales outlet, though in later years it sold Volkswagen cars. The bus is passing an Austin A40 Countryman, in reality a 10-cwt van with windows, and a 1947 Hillman Minx Phase I, while behind the bus parked outside the showrooms is an Austin A40 Devon. Following 1686 is an Austin normal control 2- to 3-ton lorry owned by George Jackson, one of many wholesalers based in the nearby Smithfield vegetable market. (J. Cockshott)

'Ready, Steady, Go!' In Digbeth on 24 May 1963, two Corporation buses and a Midland Red single-decker are lined up at the Moat Row set of traffic lights in Digbeth. 2446 (JOJ 446), a Crossley-bodied Crossley DD42/6 with a 'New Look' front, is on the right operating on the 17 route; 1515 (GOE 515), one of Birchfield Road's Daimler CVA6s, is doing a turn on the 29A service; and on the left is Midland Red's 3242 (JHA 842), a 1949 BMMO S8 with an MCCW B44F body. All are waiting for the green light to come on. It is hardly the stuff of a Grand Prix, but it would be a fair bet that the first bus across the junction was the Midland Red, though it would be a close-run thing as to which one would be second between the Crossley and the Daimler CVA6. The former had the larger 8.6-litre engine and had a 'proper' clutch and gearbox but was nearly ¾ ton heavier while the latter had a pre-select gearbox, which afforded a quicker gear change. (W. Ryan)

In May 1956, a Crossley-bodied Daimler CVG6 waits at the traffic lights at the junction with Moat Row. 3219 (MOF 219) is only eighteen months old and is, with the exception of displaying an advertisement for Schweppes Tonic, virtually in as-built condition. Closed up behind 3219 is another of the same type which is going to Pheasey on the 29A route. On the left is one of Henry Mulley's post-war Bedford OB coaches with a Duple twenty-nine-seater body; this long-established operator was based in Ixworth in Suffolk. (G. H. F. Atkins)

On the corner of Digbeth and Mill Lane was Spencer House, the headquarters of the Birmingham & Midland Motor Omnibus Company. This was part of Midland Red's Digbeth Coach Station, which was a major hub for coach services from all over the country. It was actually a bus garage with an extensive area stretching from the distant Rea Street to Mill Street which could, on a summer Saturday morning, be occupied by over thirty coaches loading up with holidaymakers. The restaurant, incidentally, sold probably the worst-tasting baked beans in the country, which spoilt breakfasts, meat pies and anything else served with them! Passing the main entrance is 2844 (JOJ 844), on its way into the city centre on the 29 route in around 1961. The bus, dating from November 1952, is a Daimler CVG6 with a Crossley H30/25R body with behind it a Hillman Minx Series III convertible. (D. R. Harvey Collection)

Six of the eight 'unfrozen' buses delivered to BCT in the first half of 1942 were Leyland Titan TD7s, fitted with Leyland H30/26R bodies that were diverted from an order for Western SM, having been allocated by the MoWT, and made up of buses whose completion had been stopped by the Government immediately after the retreat from Dunkirk, but then completed as an emergency measure. The TD7 model had the usual oil-engined Leyland 8.6-litre engines but in order to obtain the idling characteristics of a petrol-engined vehicle, they had large flywheels. This resulted in a very slow gear change, even when using the clutch stop, resulting in the model becoming unpopular with drivers. All the Birmingham ones were garaged at Perry Barr and worked on the longer services such as the Outer Circle 11 route and the 29 group of services. In around 1951, 1329 (FON 629) has just loaded up with passengers in Digbeth on the cross-city 29A route. It is at the bus stop alongside the waste ground on which Midland Red parked its Digbeth Garage allocation of buses. The bus looks distinctly tired and, with its very battered front nearside wing, looks ready for a repaint and overhaul. Unfortunately this would never happen as, later in the same year, 1329 would be in a severe accident that virtually destroyed the driver's cab, and as a result of the damage the bus would be written off. (R. Marshall Collection)

Opposite above: Passing Tomlinson's hardware shop opposite Rea Street in Digbeth is 2075 (JOJ 75), a Daimler CVD6 with a Metro-Cammell body. The bus is operating on the 29 route to Hall Green in around 1965, approximately one year before the bus was withdrawn. The advertisement on the side panels is one of the most common on Birmingham's buses at the time and was for M & B: 'It's Marvellous Beer'. 2075 is approaching the arched gateway of Miles, Druce's steel stockholder's warehouse. (D. R. Harvey Collection)

Overtaking a parked pre-war Standard Flying 14 and a 1961 Ford Zodiac 206E is Brush-bodied 1708 (HOV 708). This Leyland Titan PD2/1 is travelling out of the city centre through a somewhat deserted Digbeth and is operating on the 29A route in around 1964. The bus is passing Digbeth Civic Hall, which was opened in 16 January 1908, when it was surrounded by slums and industrial workshops. The exterior is a mixture of red brick and grey terracotta which form the ornate features of the façade and the three towers. It was an institutional church for the Congregationalists and has hosted a variety of acts, being used for boxing and wrestling events, pop concerts and even union meetings. (D. R. Harvey Collection)

Above: There is not much evidence, but this was the original site of Saxon Birmingham, with the River Rea being fordable at this point. The road entrance just visible to the left of the windscreen of the bus is Floodgate Street, which rather illustrates this location's earlier importance. 1678 (HOV 678), a Brush-bodied Leyland Titan PD2/1, is operating on the city-bound 29 route in around 1963. The only other visible vehicles are Minis, though the 1959-registered example being overtaken by the bus is a Morris Mini-Minor. Beyond this culverted river crossing is High Street, Deritend, a corruption of 'dirty end', the medieval slang word to describe the area. (R. H. G. Simpson)

Opposite above: About to pass Heath Mill Lane and the Old Crown Public House on 9 July 1966 is 2164 (JOJ 164). The pub is one of the oldest buildings to survive to the present day in Birmingham and is in Deritend. Built in 1368 as a mansion house, by 1700 it had become the first coaching inn in the town. The splendid sixteenth-century Elizabethan half-timbered, jettied frontage was spoilt by the 1862 additions to the rear of the old inn in Heath Mill Lane. The bus is working a southbound 91 service to Hall Green. Coming towards Digbeth is Midland Red BMMO D9 4861 (861KHA). (D. R. Harvey Collection)

Opposite below: 2183 (JOJ 183) was one of the first fifteen of the Leyland Titan PD2/1 buses bodied by Park Royal to have the front destination box fitted too high up, which resulted in the middle blue band not dipping beneath the aperture. This gave the buses a very distinctive look, which when combined with the standard Park Royal bodywork made the vehicles very 'unBirmingham'. These buses were either garaged at Hockley, as in this case, or Rosebery Street, both of which operated services into the Black Country, where they did not clash as much with the Birmingham standard bodies. The bus is working on the 29A route and is speeding down High Street, Bordesley, lined with mid-nineteenth-century buildings, in about 1958. (R. H. G. Simpson)

Metro-Cammell-bodied Guy Arab III Sp 2622 (JOJ 622) follows a Vauxhall Viva HB towards the city centre in High Street, Bordesley. It is being used on a 90 service in around 1973. Behind it are a line of cars and an ex-BCT Daimler Fleetline climbing over the Camp Hill flyover. It was opened on 15 October 1961 in order to improve the traffic flow at the junction of Camp Hill (A41) and Coventry Road (A45) at High Street, Bordesley. The temporary flyover was the first of its kind in UK and was erected in one weekend by J. J. Gallagher Ltd, a Bordesley Green-based contractor. It took the southbound carriageway of the A41 over the Coventry Road junction and back down onto Camp Hill. Despite the original intention, the flyover lasted for twenty-six years, before being demolished in 1987. (A. D. Broughall)

One of the last of the 'Jumbos' to remain in service, 3899 (SOE 899H) begins the descent from the crest of Camp Hill flyover when working on the 92 route to Monkspath in September 1980 only four months before its withdrawal. The 1000 Daimler Fleetline CRG6LXs ordered by BCT in 1969 had 33-foot-long Park Royal H47/33D bodies, but the provision of two doors caused the bodies to flex and show severe signs of deterioration, and the result was that they were all withdrawn prematurely. (BC Ref. Lib.)

Climbing up the steep hill in Camp Hill, having left behind High Street, Bordesley, and the future site of the Camp Hill flyover, is 1488 (GOE 488). It has already passed the Dowding & Mills electric motor rewinding factory on the hill and is approaching the junction with Bradford Street on its left, which was the original 1928 route of the 29 service into the city via the Markets area. This early post-war Daimler CVA6 is operating on the 29 service in around 1959. (F. W. York)

186 (EOG 186), a Daimler COG5 with a BRCW H30/24R body, which had entered service in January 1939, has negotiated the traffic island at Camp Hill. The tram tracks through the middle of it were originally for the Stratford Road and Warwick Road routes, which had been abandoned on 6 January 1937. The section from Bradford Street through Camp Hill to the junction with nearby Kyotts Lake Road in order to gain access to the works was retained until the final closure of the BCT tram system on 4 July 1953. All the buses have full wartime garb with masked headlights, white blackout edgings and dark grey roofs and rear domes. Bus 186 is travelling into the city on the 29A route though it has a heavily reduced destination display. It is in company with 1189 (FOF 189), on the 24 route to Warstock, and 1201 (FOF 201), operating on the 44 route to Acocks Green. (BC Ref. Lib.)

With the Ship Hotel in the background, and with blackout restrictions in full force, 1067 (CVP 167), a 1937 Daimler COG5 with a Metro-Cammell H30/24R body, passes through Camp Hill on the 29A route on its way to Hall Green in February 1944 with a reduced wartime destination blind display, which reads BALDWINS LANE & KINGSTANDING. It is being followed by an Austin Big Seven dating from 1939. The Victorian Ship Hotel public house on the corner of Camp Hill and Sandy Lane had the strange subtitle 'Prince Rupert's Headquarters – 1643', a reference to a minor skirmish between Royalist Rupert and Parliamentarians nearby in Deritend in April 1643 during the English Civil War. Confusingly, the area's name has nothing to do with Prince Rupert's 'camp', but is a corruption of Kempe Hill, named after the local fifteenth-century landowners. The photograph was taken from the wooden-braced brick parapet in Stratford Road next to Camp Hill Goods Station where the 'Please Cross Here' sign is next to a Belisha Beacon. (BC Ref. Lib.)

Coming across the junction at Camp Hill, having come from the distant Stratford Road in
Sparkbrook on 10 September 1980, is West Midlands Travel 2095 (GOG 95W). Just visible
is Camp Hill railway bridge, which for many years had been the old Midland Railways
access route into Birmingham from the south-west. 2095, a brand-new MCW Metrobus MkI
DR102/18 dating from September 1980, is coming into Birmingham on a 90 service with
the old school buildings that were once King Edward's (Camp Hill) Grammar School. (B. L.
Thompson)

Sparkbrook–Sarehole Mill
5, 6, 29, 29A, 91, and 92 Routes

From Camp Hill the bus routes travelled through Sparkbrook, Sparkhill and into Springfield, a distance of well over three miles. These were suburbs developed sequentially from the 1860s until the end of the 1890s with extensive shopping centres for each area. These numerous retail outlets supported huge areas of tunnel-backed housing on both sides of Stratford Road which as one moved away from the city improved in quality and size. Beyond Sparkhill Park and towards Springfield, the tunnel-backs rapidly gave way to superior terraced housing. There was very little industry in this area and it had the first purpose-built open space along Stratford Road at Sparkhill Park. At Springfield, which developed around the same time as the City of Birmingham Tramways last steam tram extension of 1899, the 29 and the 29A route and its successors parted company before going on different routes to their respective termini.

On 29 July 2010, 1946 (BX10 AEE) travels along Stratford Road, Sparkbrook, when operating on an inbound 5 service from Solihull railway station. This brand-new Scania Omnilink K230UB has a Polish-built Scania B43F body and has passed the Black Horse Public House, which had been built in 1880 and for many years was an Atkinson Brewery-owned hostelry on the corner of Kyotts Lake Road. Kyotts Lake Road was dominated by the Corporation tramcar repair works, where the last tramcars were broken up during July and August 1953. (D. R. Harvey)

Above: Travelling along Stratford Road in Sparkbrook on 16 August 1973 is 3205 (MOF 205). This Crossley-bodied Daimler CVG6 is operating on the 92 service to Hall Green. The bus is fitted with a very plain glass-fibre radiator grill devised by BCT in around 1966 to simplify repairs. On the right is the eighteenth-century Angel Hotel built next to the site of the old Sparkbrook tollgate, which was in use until 1872 on the Stratford Road Turnpike on the corner of Ladypool Road in order to exploit the needs of the stagecoach passengers. (E. V. Trigg)

Opposite above: Sparkbrook, in the years immediately prior to the First World War, was a thriving shopping area, with a mixture of the small mid-Victorian buildings on the left and the larger three-storey premises on the right. The two trams are both between Braithwaite Street on the right, with the newly completed Lloyds Bank on the corner, and Kyotts Lake Road. Both trams were UEC-bodied fifty-two-seater open-balconied four-wheelers. All 150 of these trams were fitted with Mountain & Gibson radial trucks, which proved troublesome and were replaced during the 1920s. The tram on the right is car 126 and is coming from Camp Hill along Stratford Road to Stoney Lane. Travelling into the city is tramcar 181 from Springfield. In front of it is the former Midland Railway's Camp Hill railway bridge and the high roof of King Edward's (Camp Hill) Grammar School. (D. R. Harvey Collection)

Opposite below: 2155 (JOJ 155), a Leyland Titan PD2/1, has a Leyland H30/26R body and was delivered in March 1949. It has just crossed the zebra crossing outside Sparkbrook Post Office in Stratford Road, Sparkbrook, and is travelling out of the city on the 29 service to Highfield Road on a summer's day in around 1957. It has begun a short climb from the Sparkbrook shopping centre and is about to reach Ladypool Road. Following 2155 is an Austin 8 hp car, which has passed Farm Road and the garage of Smith's Imperial Coaches. (D. R. Harvey Collection)

Above: On 9 June 1962, 2098 (JOJ 98), one of Yardley Wood garage's Daimler CVD6s fitted with an MCCW H30/24R body, stands in front of the Victorian row of shops between Walford Road and Poplar Road in Stratford Road, Sparkbrook. It is operating on the 29A route going to Baldwins Lane, Hall Green. These buses had similar bodies to the 2526-2625 class of Guy Arab III Specials but had minor differences particularly around the offside of the driver's cab. All of the 'New Look'-front 26-foot-long buses supplied to BCT between 1950 and 1951 could easily be identified by the shorter sliding ventilators in the first bay of the lower saloon. (G. Mead)

Opposite above: A Scania Omnilink K230 UB with a Scania B43F body leaves the bus stop in Stratford Road, Sparkbrook, when operating on the 6 route, a successor to the old 29A route on 29 July 2010. 1928 (BX10 ABU) is approaching the junction with Stoney Lane. The large office block is partly occupied by a Job Centre Plus and Birmingham Social Services. In the background is St Agatha's Church, which was consecrated in 1901 and had many Arts and Crafts features. It survived wartime bombing and a severe fire in 1957 and is the only Grade 1 listed Victorian church in Birmingham. (D. R. Harvey)

Opposite below: Passing the late nineteenth-century shops on Stratford Road between Palmerstone Road and Walford Road and approaching the Inner Circle 8 bus route is 4337 (BX02 AUT). This is in Alexander-bodied Dennis Trident 334BR low-floor double-decker which had entered service in March 2002. Behind it is 4354 (BX02 AVK), another one of the same batch. Sparkbrook began to be developed in the late 1840s with large villa-type houses and it was only some forty eyars later that the area was consumed by tunnel-back housing. The shops behind the bus date from the 1880s while just visible is Stratford Road Baptist Church, which dates from 1879. (D. R. Harvey)

Above: 3224 (MOF 224), a Crossley-bodied Daimler CVG6 dating from October 1954, is about to pull away from the rudimentary bus shelters on Stratford Road between St John's Road and Baker Street in around 1964. Perhaps the most interesting building is the one with the pair of multicoloured brick towers. This is the Salvation Army Hall, which was built in 1908 on the narrow site formerly occupied by the City of Birmingham Tramways Company as their coking depot for the Stratford Road steam trams. The buttressed spire of St John's, the Evangelist church, was built in 1905, some seventeen years after the rest of the church, and towers over the rest of the buildings on the main road. (S. N. J. White)

Opposite above: The modern-day successor to the 29A route is the 5, which follows the same route as its historic predecessor but is extended considerably from the old Baldwins Lane terminus into Shirley and then on to Solihull, where it terminates in the bus station adjacent to the railway station. 2102 (BX 12 DDO), a Volvo B7RLE with a Wright B43F body, travels along Stratford Road in Sparkbrook while being employed on an outbound 5 service on 24 November 2012. It has just passed the former Piccadilly Cinema and is about to cross the traffic lights at the junction with Warwick Road where the Mermaid public house is located. (D. R. Harvey)

Opposite below: 2174 (JOJ 174) is seen here descending the hill from Sparkhill, where the spire of St John's church is visible, to Sparkbrook, a route involving a drop of around 55 feet. This Leyland-bodied Leyland Titan PD2/1 is approaching the Mermaid Public House as it travels into the city from Baldwins Lane on the 29A route in around 1959. It is being followed by another one of Hockley garage's PD2/1s, only this time with a Park Royal body. This pair of buses is passing parked vehicles in the form of an Austin A35 van and a comparatively rare early 1950s Armstrong-Siddeley Hurricane convertible. (F. W. York)

Above: Coming towards the city on Thursday 2 May 1963 on the cross-city 29 service is 1549 (GOE 549), a MCCW-bodied Daimler CVA6. It is in Stratford Road, Sparkhill and is about to reach the junction with Showell Green Lane and the Sparkhill shopping centre. Opposite the bus are showrooms of Lincoln Street Motors, with a December 1961-registered Austin A40 Farina and a brand new Austin Mini Seven on the forecourt. The long climb from Springfield, passing Sparkhill Park, was a struggle for a fully loaded Daimler CVA6. 1549 is being followed by an Austin A40 Somerset and a much newer Austin Cambridge A60, while taking up the rear is a Guy Invincible lorry with a comparatively rare Willenhall-Coachcraft-built cab. (W. Ryan)

Opposite above: The 29A route passed Sparkhill Park into the late 1890s-built shopping centre of Springfield. This long row of shops dated from the first decade of the twentieth century and this coincided with the changeover from the CBT steam trams to the Corporation electric cars. The route then turned right into Springfield Road in front of the Birmingham Municipal Bank, leaving the 29 to continue along Stratford Road to beyond the shopping centre at the Parade, Hall Green. 1664 (HOV 664), a Brush-bodied Leyland Titan PD2/1, is making this right-turn manoeuvre in front of one of Acocks Green garage's Guy Arab IVs, 2988 (JOJ 988), which is travelling into Birmingham on the 31A route. (D. Williams)

Opposite below: Leaving Springfield Road and negotiating the very tight traffic island in College Road in around 1958 is freshly repainted 2170 (JOJ 170) working on a 29A service. The houses, Board Primary School and the solitary shop in College Road all dated from the last decade of the nineteenth century and virtually marked the end of the city's pre-First World War expansion. Hockley-based 2170, the first of the class to be withdrawn, on 31 May 1967, has come from the Baldwins Lane terminus at the boundary with Shirley and will travel through Sparkhill on its way into the city centre before heading to Kingstanding and the Pheasey Estate in Aldridge. (F. W. York)

Above: Birmingham's entire 250 'New Look'-front Daimler CVG6s were bodied by Crossley Motors. Both the 1952 JOJ-registered and the 1954 MOF-registered buses were operated by Yardley Wood garage and were stalwarts of the long route between Baldwins Lane and Pheasey Estate for over twenty years, lasting well into WMPTE days. 2859 (JOJ 859) has just turned into Sarehole Road from Cole Bank Road on the 90 route on 16 May 1974. The R symbol on the lamp post being passed by the MGB GT car signified that Sarehole Road was part of Birmingham's Outer Ring Road. (E. V. Trigg)

Opposite above: Having just picked up passengers in Wake Green Road on the border with Moseley is a 72-seater Wright-bodied Volvo B7TL, 4657 (BX54 XRB), which had entered service in November 2004. This National Express West Midlands double-decker is being used on the 5 route to Baldwins Lane and Solihull on Tuesday 5 March 2013 and is descending the hill towards Sarehole Road, where it will turn left to pass Sarehole Mill. (D. R. Harvey)

Opposite below: Passing Sarehole Mill in Sarehole Road, Hall Green, is Crossley-bodied Daimler CVG6 3115 (MOF 115). This section of Sarehole Road is also part of the 11, Outer Circle bus route. This bus is working on the 91 route on 21 October 1974 when in WMPTE ownership. 3115 entered service as one of the allocation of buses replacing the Erdington group of trams on 4 July 1953. Sarehole Mill is first mentioned in 1542 as a corn mill on the River Cole, which with its tributaries once boasted around five mills, of which Sarehole is the only survivor. By 1762 it was being used for metal workingm with the young Matthew Boulton using the mill as a tenant for rolling metal to make buttons before he established the Soho Manufactory at Handsworth. In 1775 it was said to be a 'complete new corn mill, well supplied with water'. Most of the surviving buildings date from that period. There were two waterwheels by 1807, one being for corn and the other wheel used mainly for metalwork such as blade grinding. A steam engine had been installed and a chimney added to the building by 1873, but the mill remained a corn mill and was in use until 1919. The buildings were restored during the 1960s and are now open to the public as a working mill. It still grinds its own flour, which is baked on the premises. Sarehole Mill provided the inspiration for J. R. R. Tolkien's mill in *The Hobbit*. (C. C. Thornburn)

Springfield–Highfield Road and Shirley
5, 6, 29, 90 and 92 Routes

At Springfield the 29 route continued beyond Collge Road and across the River Cole Bridge and up the hill in Stratford Road to Hall Green where after crossing the former Great Western Railway's North Warwickshire Railway line to Stratford, the route continued to the start of the dual carriageway built and used for Birmingham Corporation penultimate tramway extension of 1928 to Hall Green. The 29 route turned right at this point and travelled along Highfield Road along the tree-lined dual carriageway lined with the semi-detached interwar housing as far as Yardley Wood Station. Back in Springfield, the 29A route turned right into Springfield Road which marked the end of Victorian development in Stratford Road. The route entered a highly desirable area developed in the Edwardian period in Wake Green Road on the border with Moseley. It then turned left into Cole Bank Road where it briefly followed the Outer Circle 11 bus route and stopped outside the eighteenth-century Sarehole Mill standing in the River Cole. After turning right into Sarehole Road, the 29A meandered its way through Hall Green in a suburb developed with private housing in the 1930s. The route then travelled by way of Robin Hood Lane before going by way of Kedleston Road to the terminus at the Baldwin Public House at the Birmingham boundary with Solihull. After us Deregulation the former 91 route had become the 5 route and was extended through Shirley along A34 Stratford Road on the 5 service and then on to Solihull Station.

Above: The climb out of the flood plain of the River Cole, up the hill from the College Arms Public House dating from 1913 at the junction with Shaftesmoor Lane to the long row of shops on The Parade in Hall Green, was surprisingly steep. The hill took the road from 379 feet above sea level up to the summit at 428 feet at Reddings Lane. In 1970, not long before the 29 route was replaced as a cross-city route, 2890 (JOJ 890), a Crossley-bodied Daimler CVG6, ascends the hill with a gathering queue of following cars led by an Austin A35 car. (D. R. Harvey Collection)

Opposite: An immaculately painted car, 571, climbs up the hill from Shaftesmoor Lane when working out of town on the 18 route to the Hall Green city boundary in October 1936. This UEC-built sixty-two-seater tram of 1914, mounted on Mountain & Gibson Burnley bogies, had 40 hp Dick, Kerr motors. The tram had its balconies enclosed in 1927 and was fitted at the same time with upholstered seats. It was one of twenty-two of the 512 class to operate out of Highgate Road depot, and except for its low-horsepower motors giving it a slow top speed it entered the 1930s as an up-to-date, economical and efficient mover of passengers. Following the tram is a Morris Twelve and an Austin Ten-Four, while one of the bus routes that overran the 'main-line' tram route before branching off, the 32 route, is being worked by an early Daimler COG5 of the AOB-registered series, distinguishable by its lack of a cream-painted waist rail. (W. A. Camwell)

Above: Although not regular performers on the Highfield Road services, 3891 (SOE 891H) turns across the former tramway central reservation in Stratford Road and into Highfield Road, while close behind it is a Ford Capri car. This was the site of the tramway terminus of the 18 service from 31 May 1914 until 2 April 1928 when it was extended to the city boundary. On the far side of the dual carriageway is the Bull's Head Public House, which is a delightful former hotel that dates from the 1830s. The bus is one of 100 33-foot-long Daimler Fleetlines with two-door Park Royal bodies ordered by Birmingham City Transport in 1969 but mostly delivered after West Midlands PTE had taken over on 1 October 1969. (D. R. Harvey Collection)

Opposite above: On 18 September 1965, 1699 (HOV 699), the first of Perry Barr garage's allocation of the Brush-bodied Leyland Titan PD2/1s, was turning into Highfield Road from Stratford Road. It was almost in sight of the nearby terminus but managed to overturn when making the manoeuvre in front of the large mock-Tudor shops at the junction of Stratford Road and Highfield Road. Although the chassis, revealed as the bus lay on its side, was in excellent condition, the offside of the Brush body was extensively damaged. This accident resulted in the almost immediate withdrawal of 1699. (Birmingham Mail)

Opposite below: Standing at the bus stop outside the row of large mock-Tudor shops in Highfield Road is Daimler Fleetline CRG6LX/33 3895 (SOE 895H). It is facing the junction with Stratford Road when working the 29 route as a service extra. These Park Royal-bodied buses were nicknamed 'Jumbos' because of their large seating capacity of eighty. This bus was delivered on 8 October 1969 but because of weaknesses in the construction of their double-doored bodies, all of them had been withdrawn by 1981, with 3895 going in September 1980. It was sold to the Essex dealer, Ensign of Grays, along with seventeen others, but unlike nearly all the others, it was deemed not worthy of resale and was promptly broken up. (D. R. Harvey Collection)

In the process of turning around the central reservation in Highfield Road at the terminus of the 29 route is one of the attractive-looking Crossley-bodied Crossley DD42/6s, 2375 (JOJ 375), dating from March 1950. Hauling these buses around tight turns was hard work and the exposed-radiator Crossleys could be especially hard work for the driver. It is noticeable, however, that the driver is using the correct 'push-pull' method of turning the steering wheel. Behind the bus is a row of 1920s bungalows, while coming down Highfield Road is a 1937 Ford 7W Tudor saloon with the characteristic 'three-hole' radiator grill. (W. A. Camwell)

Above: Towards the end of its life, 2127 (JOJ 127) stands at the Highfield Road terminus with the turning circle in Paradise Lane beyond the green-painted bus shelter, facing Stratford Road with behind it the end of the dual carriageway and Yardley Wood Station. The bus is a 1951 Daimler CVD6 with a Metro-Cammell body and would be withdrawn in July 1966. The array of street furniture associated with this terminus is surprising. There is a bus stop with a litter bin and what might be a timetable, though BCT rarely displayed timetable information to the general public. Next is the Bundy Clock to record departure times and beyond that the bus shelter and a rather substantial double-sided bench. The 29 and the later 29 southbound cross-city service from Kingstanding to Hall Green and its northbound 30 route equivalent were eventually removed from timetables on 28 February 1971, leaving the 29 to become a Hall Green local feeder route to the College Arms, Springfield. Even this was reduced to peaks only before being withdrawn in 1979. (D. R. Harvey Collection)

Opposite above: Pulling away from the penultimate bus stop in Highfield Road, Hall Green, on 22 July 1931 is 2½-year-old bus 318 (VP 1182), working on the 29 route towards the terminus near Yardley Wood railway station. 318 was an ADC 507 with an outside-staircase Short H24/26R body. This tree-lined suburbia should have been the preserve of the tram, as in cities like Liverpool and Sheffield, but in Birmingham buses gradually began to dominate and it was the bus routes to newly developed housing estates off the main Stratford Road tram routes that really put paid to that group of tram services. In the 1920s dual carriageways such as Highfield Road's central reservation were built to take tram tracks at a future date, but the rapid improvements to the bus fleet meant that this policy was never carried out, which is why the young lady on the left, on her way home to her almost-new three-bedroom semi-detached house, has got off a bus, not a tram. (BC Ref. Lib.)

Hall Green – Shirley
90 and 92 Routes

This extended the former 37 bus route through Shirley's shopping centre to Cranmore Boulevard, Monkspath opposite the Joseph Lucas Research factory. The 92 route was extended in 1986 to Solihull Station.

The existing tram route had been extended by around three-quarters of a mile along reserved-track tramway to the city boundary at Hall Green from opposite Highfield Road on 2 April 1928. This was the penultimate route to be lengthened, but the Stratford Road group of tram services was abandoned in January 1937 due to bus routes overriding the tram route before branching off the main road to access newer housing areas. Tram 585 stands at the Hall Green city boundary on 7 December 1936, one month before the closure of the 18 route. The tram entered service in December 1914 and had a pair of Burnley-type maximum-traction bogies coupled to Dick, Kerr DKA 40 hp motors and a sixty-two-seat UEC body, originally with open balconies. Variously re-motored, re-bogied and vestibuled, 585 lasted in service until February 1952. (R. T. Wilson)

When the 37 route was abandoned on 28 February 1971, it was replaced by the 90 service, which travelled northwards across the city to Pheasey. Correspondingly, the 92 became the new number for buses travelling from Pheasey to the Hall Green boundary with Shirley. At the same time, the 29 and 30 routes ceased as cross-city routes and effectively the original Highfield Road service was abandoned some forty-three years after it had first been introduced. With its destination blind already set to 90 for the return northbound journey, 3173 (MOF 173), a Crossley-bodied Daimler CVG6, is standing in the same turning-back point at the Hall Green city boundary that was used by the old 37 route. The buses crossed the former tramway central reservation in order to return to the city and clocked in at a Bundy Clock next to the former tram shelter, to the right of the bus. (D. R. Harvey Collection)

The use of the Birmingham/Shirley boundary was something of an anachronism as passengers wanted to travel directly from the city centre to Shirley. All this area was administered by Centro and the buses operated by WMPTE and so, on 6 April 1975, this anomaly was ended. The 92 service was extended beyond the Birmingham city boundary through Shirley to the junction with Cranmore Boulevard at Monkspath. 4581 (GOG 581N), a Park Royal-bodied Daimler Fleetline CRG6LX, had entered service just one month after this extension to the 92 route had taken place. The bus stands in the lay-by on the main A34 Stratford Road opposite Cranmore Boulevard, almost outside the impressive headquarters of Joseph Lucas, the aerospace and vehicle electrical components manufacturer. (Travel Lens)

Robin Hood Lane–Solihull
5, 29A, 90 and 91 Routes

The 6 route was developed by National Express West Midlands and replaced the former 92 route along Stratford Road through Hall Green and Shirley before turning into Cranmore Boulevard and Widney Manor Railway Station to terminate at Solihull Station alongside the 5 route.

The railway bridge over Robin Hood Lane was plated with a clearance height of 14 feet 9 inches in 1965. The railway line carried by the bridge originated as the independent Birmingham & North Warwickshire Railway under the auspices of the Great Western Railway. It opened in 1908, providing a direct link between Tyseley, Bearley and Stratford. It was part of a final surge of main-line railway building in Britain, which ended with the First World War. 1660 (HOV 660), a Brush-bodied Leyland Titan PD2/1, has just passed beneath the railway bridge when travelling on an outbound 91 service going towards Baldwins Lane. This bus is one of nineteen of the class of 100 that had chassis built in 1947. (A. D. Broughall)

Operating on the 5 route on 5 March 2013 is 4650 (BX54 XRG). This 2004-vintage Volvo B7TL has a Wright H43/27F body and these Yardley Wood-garage-based buses had become the standard double-deckers on this route. By now the official height of the railway bridge had been reduced to 14 feet 3 inches, which is ironic as the double-deckers passing beneath the bridge on the 6 service are around 3 inches higher than the standard former Birmingham City Transport buses which famously operated on the 29A service. (D. R. Harvey)

Travelling down the hill towards the railway bridge in Robin Hood Lane on 5 March 2013 is another Wright-bodied Volvo B7TL whose styling detail was quickly nicknamed 'Nokia' after the rounded front of the then-current mobile phone. 4675 (BX54 XPV), dating from November 2004, passes the typical line of inter-war semi-detached houses which dominate the urban landscape of the area between Hall Green and Billesley when operating on the 5 service. These buses, with their distinctive styling, seated only seventy-two passengers when compared to the seventy-seven on the contemporary Alexander-bodied Dennis Enviro 400s. (D. R. Harvey)

Above: It was still raining on 2 April 1989 by the time 2489 (JOJ 489), the preserved 1950-vintage Crossley-bodied Crossley DD42/6, arrived at the Baldwins Lane terminus on its tour of BCT routes. Behind the bus stop is the Art Deco-style Baldwin public house. It was opened on 11 December 1936 and derived its name from a family of sixteenth-century farmers named Baldwyn. This was the terminus of the 29A route from its introduction on 1 January 1936 until renumbered after 29 November 1964 by Birmingham City Transport. After this date it became the cross-city service 90/91, which ran from Pheasey via the city centre and to the Baldwin as service 91, returning as service 90. On 6 April 1975 West Midlands PTE amended this numbering slightly, such that the 90 ran from Pheasey to the Baldwin Public House in both directions. The route became renumbered and extended to Solihull station as the 5 in October 1986, while at the same time the service through Shirley was extended through Widney Manor as the 6. (D. R. Harvey Collection)

Opposite below: Standing outside the Baldwin public house at the terminus of the 29A route in Hall Green in around 1950 is 1051 (CVP 151), a Daimler COG5 which had entered service in August 1937. The bus had swapped Metro-Cammell bodies with 1027 in April 1948, which was one of ninety bodies renovated by Samlesbury Engineering. Unfortunately this did not, in this case, extend the life of the bus as it was involved in an accident, which resulted in its premature withdrawal at the end of January 1952. Drawn up at the terminus behind the pre-war bus is 1500 (GOE 500), a Daimler CVA6 dating from 1947. (R. A. Mills)

Above: Facing the Solihull boundary in Newborough Road to the left, 296 (HOJ 396) is about to do a 360° turn around the traffic island in Baldwins Lane. 296 was the second prototype Leyland PD2 chassis, with the number EX2. It was completed at the end of July 1947 and given the chassis number 470848. 296 had the new large 9.8-litre 0.600 engine and a Leyland PD1-style body altered around the front of the cab and the offside mudguard. The bus was given the next fleet number after the last of the 1939 batch of Metro-Cammell-bodied Leyland Titan TD6cs, thus becoming the only post-war bus not to be numbered in the main fleet sequence. 296 entered service on Monday 29 September 1947, sporting a pair of large, brass-rimmed PDI-type headlights. This bus was allocated to Yardley Wood garage for all its life, but it was only occasionally used on the 29/29A services. Although it looked like a member of Hockley garage's 2131 class, it did have numerous detail differences, such as the positioning of the half drop windows in both saloons. It also it had to be manned by tall conductors as the platform bell was difficult to reach. 296 was the first post-war vehicle to operate for twenty years, although it only achieved 312,000 miles in service. Here it is at the Bundy Clock at the Baldwins Lane terminus in around 1966 and it is displaying a destination suggesting that it will be returning empty back to garage. (D. R. Harvey Collection)

Opposite above: When the 29A group of services was most recently renumbered to 5, the service was also extended to Shirley and then on to Solihull. On Saturday 24 November 2012, picking up passengers on a miserable day outside the Baldwin public house, is 4655 (BX54 XRZ), a Wright-bodied Volvo B7TL. Since 1989, the terminus at Baldwins Lane had acquired a much-needed enclosed bus shelter, while the pub sign has been updated with a very 1930s-style font. The recent use of these Volvo B7TL buses on both the 5/6 route and the 33 service from the city centre almost harks back to when the 29A route was a cross-city route and was worked by Brush-bodied Leyland Titan PD2/1s from Perry Barr and Yardley Wood garages. (D. R. Harvey)

Opposite below: Bus 3216 (MOF 216) waits at the Baldwins Lane Bundy Clock at the terminus of the 29A route in around 1963. This 1954-vintage Crossley-bodied Daimler CVG6 is about to be overtaken by a 1951-registered Bradford van – these were built by Jowett of Bradford with a flat, twin, 1005-cc engine from 1946 until 1954. The bus shelter was of the wartime utilitarian type, which unless the rain was falling vertically, afforded virtually no protection in inclement weather for intending passengers. (A. D. Broughall)

Above: Travelling through Shirley along A34 Stratford Road on the 6 service towards Solihull on 24 November 2012 is 4653 (BX54 XPR), a Volvo B7TL with a Wright H43/29F. There are many shops and businesses in this affluent suburb of Solihull – they line the route for over a mile. Shirley developed slowly as a small village on the Stratford Road, called Shirley Street, through the settlement. Between 1725 and 1872, Stratford Road was a turnpike, and after the road lost its gated status, in the late nineteenth and early twentieth century Shirley grew rapidly as wealthier people were able to move out of Birmingham, helped by the opening of the railway in 1908. (D. R. Harvey)

Opposite above: Parked at the bus stop opposite Solihull railway station in 2003 is 4333 (BX02 AUF). This Dennis Trident SFD334 has an Alexander H47/28F body and had entered service in March 2002. The bus is operating on the 6 route directly along Stratford Road back to Birmingham. These Dennis Tridents were the mainstay of the 5/6 route corridor for around six years and provided an excellent record of reliability. Behind it is Mark II MCW Metrobus 2606 (POG 606Y), which has just arrived via the 37 Warwick Road route from the city. (A. E. Hall)

Opposite below: Standing at the 5 route terminus at Solihull Station on 13 June 2012 is 1935 (BX10 ACV). The bus is a Scania Omnilink K230UB with a Scania B43F, and entered service in April 2010. Since the delivery of these Scania buses, they have been used by Yardley Wood garage in conjunction with Volvo B7TL double-deckers on the 5 route via Baldwins Lane, though their appearance on the more direct 6 service is less common. Despite their length, the Scania body only seats forty-three passengers, which is the National Express West Midlands standard for a full-sized single-decker, although there is considerable space for standing passengers, prams and wheelchairs. (D. R. Harvey)

Out to the West

33 and 34 Routes

The former 34 route along Hagley Road to Quinton was replaced by the 34 route, whereupon it was linked to the 33 bus service as a cross-city service.

This was the western half of peak hour cross-city service along Hagley Road to Quinton at the terminus it shared at the City boundary in Hagley Road West. The route left the City by way of Navigation Street, John Bright Street before climbing the steep hill in Holloway Head. This former well-to-do Georgian developed area had been over run with mid-Victorian back-to-back housing and this was not properly cleared until the development of the Lee Bank Central Development Area begun in the late 1950s. Passing Davenport's Brewery and the Accident Hospital in Bath Row, the route turned along Islington Row and reached the start of Hagley Road at Five Ways. Little over half a mile from the appalling housing in Lee Bank, the Edgbaston addresses along Hagley Road and Calthorpe Road could not have been a greater contrast in urban living. The Hagley Road corridor out of the city on its western approaches was part of the heavily protected Calthorpe Estate and contained some of the most expensive and desirable houses in Birmingham. This was the penultimate tram route along a major arterial route to be opened and was strongly objected to by the Anstruther Gough Calthorpe family who did not want Hagley Road to have the 'unsightly electric tramway overhead' spoiling this most select road. No matter BCT opened the tram route on 5 September 1913 to the Kings Head Public House at the Bearwood boundary, but in an attempt to placate the local residents, ran a First Class tram service from Fountain Road just west of the L&NWR's Hagley Road Station. Given a route number 34 during the First World War, the service was not successful and on 9 August 1930 it was converted to buses. In 1909, Quinton had a referendum about its water supply and the eastern Birmingham side voted to become part of the city and obtain water from the newly opened Elan Valley Reservoirs owned by Birmingham Council in Central Wales. The area was around 650 feet above sea level, had poor quality farmland and like Kingstanding on the other end of the 33/34 bus route was ripe for urban municipal expansion. The First World War and the Depression delayed any further development until the 1930s and as a result the 34 route was extended from Quinton via College Road to Ridgacre Road.

In Navigation Street in August 1954 is 2117 (JOJ 117). This Metro-Cammell-bodied Daimler CVD6 'New Look'-front bus, which had entered service from Perry Barr garage on 1 July 1951, is still wearing its aluminium decorative hub caps as it travels out of the city centre on the 34 route. It is displaying the destination QUINTON VIA SIX WAYS & HOLLOWAY HEAD. Behind the bus, travelling away from Stephenson Street, is a Mitchells & Butlers Austin K4 Loadstar brewery lorry and the towering presence of the Queen's Hotel. The original hotel had been opened in 1854 with sixty bedrooms and was extended to eighty-six rooms in 1859. In 1911 it had reached bursting point and a new extension was built with a further ninety-four bedrooms, but even this was not enough and in 1926 the whole building was enlarged by adding a further two storeys. This was Birmingham's premier hotel, but when the plans for the 1960s rebuilding of the station were announced, there was no room for a replacement. It was closed on New Year's Eve 1965 and demolished. (G. F. Douglas courtesy A. D. Packer)

Above: Passing the remains of St Thomas's Church in Bath Row is Corporation Daimler CVA6 1508 (GOE 508), working to Quinton on the 34 route in around 1959. St Thomas's Church had its foundation stone laid by the Bishop of Worcester on 22 October 1826 and was built in the neoclassical, rather than the more usual Gothic, style being consecrated exactly three years later. On the night of 11 December 1940, all but the fine tower and classical west portico of St Thomas's was destroyed by German bombs. The church was never rebuilt and it survives as a peace garden. At the top of Holloway Head, behind the bus, are grim, mid-nineteenth-century three-storey back-to-back courtyard houses. (F. W. York)

Opposite above: Turning out of St Martin's Street into Islington Row in 1959 is 2375 (JOJ 375). This route was part of the minor route alterations introduced on 11 December 1936. This Perry Barr-allocated Crossley DD42/6 is going towards Five Ways on the 34 route. About half of the buses used on the cross-city 34 service were supplied by Quinton garage, so to see an exposed-radiator Crossley was unusual as they had synchromesh gearboxes. As Quinton's drivers were not usually passed out to drive buses with manual gearboxes, if there was a problem Quinton's drivers were unable to drive them, at least officially. (D. R. Harvey Collection)

Opposite below: Loading up at the utility bus shelters in Hagley Road at Five Ways opposite the old King Edward's School buildings on Christmas Eve 1949 is 1238 (FOF 238). This bus is on its way to Quinton on the cross-city 34 route from Kingstanding. This Daimler COG5 was unique in that it was the only one to have a Park Royal H30/24R body. This bus service replaced the 34 tram on 11 August 1930, making it the third Birmingham tram route to be abandoned. The replacement bus took the route from Navigation Street, by way of Holloway Head and Islington Row, to Five Ways, Hagley Road and the outer terminus at the Kings Head, Lordswood Road. 1238's body had the thinnest front corner pillar of any pre-war body mounted on a Daimler COG5, a rather square destination aperture and a curved profile to the area above the number plate. Inside, it was the only bus in the fleet to have metal-capped window pillars rather than the normal varnished wood, but otherwise it was perhaps the most modern-looking body on a Birmingham COG5. (J. Cull)

Birmingham, The Oratory.   Ana Series: 031.

In the early 1920s, one of Rosebery Street depot's 512 class cars is working the 34 route towards the city. The tram has left the Ivy Bush junction and has now entered the half-mile of straight track that will take the route to Five Ways. The route-numbering scheme was adopted in 1915 and the canopy roller-blind route boxes were installed after 1917, although it took a number of years to re-equip all the tramcar fleet. The tram is passing the Roman Catholic Oratory Church of the Immaculate Conception, the dome of which can be seen behind the Gothic-style church house on the corner of Plough & Harrow Road. The church, largely hidden by the school buildings, was built in the Italian Renaissance style between 1903 and 1906 as a memorial to Cardinal John Henry Newman. (Commercial postcard)

The Hagley Road tram service to the Birmingham boundary at the Kings Head was never wanted by the residents of the wealthy Calthorpe Estate as it would compete with the 'Harborne Flyer', a short branch-line railway service from New Street, and they also objected to the 'unsightly' tram overhead. Despite protestations and even representation from the local Edgbaston Member of Parliament, Neville Chamberlain, the route was opened on 5 September 1913. In order to placate the residents and increase its popularity, Birmingham Corporation introduced first-class trams on the service in February 1914, but this was abandoned in the following May. Here, Car 582 is displaying the notice that there are DOUBLE FARES ONLY INSIDE, showing that it is working as a first-class tram, a service which did not start at the Kings Head Public House, but at Fountain Road some half a mile short of the normal terminus. The route was finally converted to buses on 9 August 1930, as the third BCT tram route to be abandoned. (A. D. Packer)

Above: Just into WMPTE ownership, Daimler Fleetline CRG6LX 3359 (359 KOV), fitted with the first design of Park Royal bodywork with a somewhat uninspired flat frontal appearance, travels towards the Kings Head Public House when operating on the 34 route. The BCT Standard bus is working on the Outer Circle 11 bus route and is about to turn left into Barnsley Road. In the window of Cranmore Brothers car showroom is one of the recently introduced revolutionary Range Rover station wagons, while passing the showrooms is an Austin A60 Cambridge saloon. (A. J. Douglas)

Opposite above: One of Perry Barr garage's 1958 allocation of seven Daimler COG5s, 1115 (CVP 215), unloads its passengers outside The Hollybush public house in Hagley Road West in around 1960, working on the long cross-city 34 service from Kingstanding to Quinton. On the other side of the dual carriageway is the Hollybush shopping parade. About to overtake the bus is a Morris J2 van. 1115 received the body from 1083 in 1948 when it came in for its first major post-war overhaul, and like many of these vehicles it was sent to Samlesbury Engineering, of Samlesbury near Blackburn, for renovation. Like all the COG5s that were put back into front-line service in 1958, 1115 has been given the Tyburn Road works treatment, and although it only remained in service until the end of December 1959, it looks extremely smart except for its rather dull radiator. (A. D. Broughall)

Opposite below: Parked at the head of a line of parked buses at the Hagley Road West, Quinton, terminus of the 9 and 34 routes in around 1972 is 4231 (YOX 231K). This MCW-bodied Daimler Fleetline CRG6LX, built for WMPTE in July 1972, is waiting to leave from this most westerly terminus on the 33 route across the city to Finchley Road, Kingstanding. Behind is 3436 (436 KOV), another earlier Daimler Fleetline with a Park Royal body, later to be purchased for preservation in 1981, which is operating on the 9 route. 3101 (MOF 101), the penultimate Guy Arab IV in the Birmingham Corporation fleet, is parked at the bus stop with its bonnet lifted up as though there might be something wrong with it. (D. R. Harvey Collection)

History of the routes

This table of services, dates, routes and closures omits wartime evening cuts and corresponding termini alterations as well a certain minor alterations throughout the period. After De-regulation, services especially in the Solihull area were frequently modified for only a short period and are not included below for sake of clarity.

Service No	Start date	Route taken and alterations	Closure or replacement	Notes
25 *Peak Hours only*	17/12/1934	Finchley Road, Kingstanding via Ellerton Road, Warren Farm Road, Kingstanding Road, Aldridge Road, Birchfield Road, Heathfield Road, Villa Road, Hamstead Road, Soho Hill, Hockley Brook, Hockley Hill, Great Hampton Street and Constitution Hill to Snow Hill, Bull Street, Corporation Street, New Street, Lower Temple Street, Navigation Street, Hill Street, Hurst Street, Bromsgrove Street, Moat Row, Bradford Street to Camp Hill. *Then as 29 to Highfield Road, Hall Green.*		
	17/6/1936	*Diverted northward* from Hurst Street via Hill Street and Victoria Square to New Street.		
	23/5/1938	*Markets diversion* between 6.45 a.m. and 9.30 a.m. on weekdays from Bradford Street via Rea Street, Moseley Street, Sherlock Street and Hurst Street to Hill Street.		
	25/9/39	*Cut back* Kingstanding to Fox Hollies Road only.	City to Hall Green *discontinued*	*Never an all day service*
	5/10/1942	*Cut back* Kingstanding, (Finchley Road) to City Loop only as peak periods only.	Route abandoned	
	28/2/1971 ?	Subsumed into 33 and 91 timetables		

29	6/2/1928	Boar's Head, Aldridge via Birchfield Road, Six Ways, Alma Street, Summer Lane, Snow Hill, Bull Street, Corporation Street, New Street, Lower Temple Street, Navigation Street, Hill Street, Hurst Street, Bromsgrove Street, Moat Row, Bradford Street, Camp Hill and Stratford Road to Highfield Road.		
	26/8/1929	*Diverted from* Birchfield Road, via Heathfield Road, Villa Road, Hamstead Road, Soho Hill, Hockley Brook, Hockley Hill, Great Hampton Street and Constitution Hill to Snow Hill.		
	5/11/1930	*Extended from* Boar's Head via College Road, Kingstanding Road and Warren Farm Road to Ellerton Road.		
	24/8/1931	*Diverted from* Kingstanding Road to Kings Road, (Kingstanding Circle)		
	5/6/1933	**One-way City Centre scheme; southward** from Snow Hill via Colmore Row, New Street and Stephenson Street. **Northward** via Lower Temple Street, New Street, Corporation Street, Bull Street and Snow Hill.		
	3/7/1933	*Diverted southwards* from New Street via Ethel Street to Navigation Street.		
	4/11/1934	*Diverted northwards* from Camp Hill via Bordesley, Deritend, Digbeth, Bull Ring, New Street, Corporation Street, and Bull Street to Snow Hill. *Diverted southwards* from Snow Hill via Bull Street, High Street, Bull Ring, Digbeth, Deritend, Bordesley to Camp Hill.		
	17/8/1936	*Diverted southwards* from Snow Hill via Steelhouse Lane, Corporation Street, Bull Street to High Street.		
	25/9/1939	*War-time cut back* Kingstanding to Fox Hollies Road only.		*War-time cut back*
	19/8/1940	*Extended from* Kingstanding, via Lambeth Road to Collingwood Drive.		
	21/4/1941	*Cut back* to Kings Road, Kingstanding, (Circle). *Replaced by 29A route.*		
	28/1/1946	*Reintroduced to* Highfield Road, (Yardley Wood Station).		
	15/4/1946	**Night Service NS 29** from Bull Street to Kings Road, Kingstanding Circle.		
	25/8/1947	**Discontinued** and replaced by NS 29A.		

	13/11/1960	Use of St Martin's Circus, Bull Ring.		
	29/11/1964	29 *used for southward journeys* from Kingstanding to Hall Green.	*Discontinued renumbered* for northbound journeys as 30 from Hall Green to Kingstanding	
	28/2/1971	Reduced service from Yardley Wood Station via Stratford Road to College Arms, Shaftesmoor Lane	**Withdrawn** 7/1979	

34	11/8/1930	**Tramway replacement 34 route.** Navigation Street via John Bright Street, Holloway Head, Hagley Road to "Kings Head". Return via Holloway Head and Suffolk Street to Navigation Street.		
	12/1/1931	**Linked with 33 route** via Navigation Street and Lower Temple Street.		
	2/12/1931	*Extended from* King's Head via Hagley Road to Quinton.		
	3/7/1933	*Diverted from* New Street via Ethel Street to Navigation Street on outbound route.		
	18/2/1935	Extended from Quinton via College Road to Ridgacre Road.		
	17/8/1936	*Diverted southward* from Lower Loveday Street via Corporation Street, Bull Street and Colmore Row to New Street. *Diverted northward* from Navigation Street, Victoria Square, New Street, Corporation Street, Bull Street and Steelhouse Lane to Loveday Street.		
	11/12/1936	*Diverted outward* from Five Ways via Harborne Road and Highfield Road to Hagley Road.		
	14/7/1937	*Diverted* from Hagley Road West via Ridgacre Lane to College Road.		
	25/9/1939	*Cut back* to operate on at peak periods on weekdays.		*Never reinstated as an all day service*
	21/10/1942	*Diverted from* Five Ways via Islington Row to Bath Row.		
	28/2/1949	Diverted from Suffolk Street via Swallow Street to Hill Street and Victoria Square.		

	1/1/1950	*Diverted southwards* from Six Ways, Newtown Row, Lancaster Street, Lancaster Place, Stafford Street, Dale End, High Street, New Street, Stephenson Place and Stephenson Street to Navigation Street, John Bright Street and Holloway Head.		
	24/5/1964	*Diverted southwards* from Navigation Street via Hill Street, Station Street and John Bright Street to Holloway Head.		
	29/4/1968	*Diverted from* High Street via St Martin's Circus, Smallbrook Ringway to Holloway Circus.		
	5/12/1976?	**Abandoned** in favour of 130 route		

33	18/8/1930	Ellerton Road, Kingstanding via Warren Farm Road, Kingstanding Road, College Road, Aldridge Road, Birchfield Road, Six Ways, Alma Street, Summer Lane, Lower Loveday Street, Loveday Street and City Loop *(Corporation Street, Bull Street, Colmore Row, New Street, Corporation Street.)*		
	12/1/1931	**Linked with 34 route** via New Street, Lower Temple Street and Navigation Street.		
	2/1/1933	*Extended from* Ellerton Road to Finchley Road.		
	17/8/1936	*Diverted southward* from Lower Loveday Street via Corporation Street, Bull Street and Colmore Row to New Street.		
	11/12/1936	*Diverted inwards* from Five Ways via Broad Street, St Martin's Street and Tennant Street to Islington Row.		
	25/9/1939	*Cut back* Bull Street to Kingstanding linked on peak time weekdays only.		
	1/1/1950	*City terminus altered* from Bull Street to Martineau Street. *Diverted northward* via Corporation Street, Bull Street, Steelhouse Lane, Lancaster Place, Lancaster Street, Newtown Row to Six Ways. *Diverted southwards* from Six Ways, Newtown Row, Lancaster Street, Lancaster Place, Stafford Street, Dale End and to Martineau Street.		
	16/10/1960	*City terminus altered* from Martineau Street to Union Street.		

	29/4/1968	*Diverted from* Holloway Circus, Smallbrook Ringway, St Martin's Circus and New Street.		
	26/10/1986	*Extended from* Finchley Road via Kings Road, Kingstanding Circle, Bandywood Road, and Lambeth Road to Collingwood Drive.	Incorporating 90 route.	

29A	1/1/1936	Kingstanding Circle to City and Stratford Road *using 29 route*. Then via Springfield Road, Wake Green Road, Colebank Road, Sarehole Road, Robin Hood Lane, Kedleston Road, Scribers Lane to Baldwins Lane.		
	17/8/1936	*Diverted southwards* from Snow Hill via Steelhouse Lane, Corporation Street, Bull Street to High Street.		
	25/9/1939	*Diverted northward* from Navigation Street, Victoria Square, New Street, Corporation Street, Bull Street and Steelhouse Lane to Loveday Street.		
	21/4/1941	*Extended from* Kingstanding, via Lambeth Road to Collingwood Drive, Pheasey.		
	25/8/1947	**Night Service 29A** extended 29 route from Kingstanding Road to Queslett Road.		
	13/11/1960	Use of St Martin's Circus, Bull Ring.		
	29/11/1964	**Renumbering.**	*Discontinued. Renumbered* 90 for northbound journeys from Baldwins Lane to Pheasey. Renumbered 91 for southbound journeys from Pheasey to Baldwins Lane.	Service from both outer termini to City only showed 90 in both directions
98	1/4/1968	**Express Service.** New Street, Bull Street, Snow Hill, Summer Lane, Six Ways, Aston, Birchfield Road, Perry Barr underpass, Aldridge Road, Kingstanding Road to Kingstanding Circle.		

90	28/2/1971	*Northbound only* to City from Baldwins Lane or Stratford Road, Hall Green		
	1/6/1975		Converted to OMO	
	28/10/1986	*Renumbered* 33 and re-routed from Finchley Road via Kings Road, Kingstanding Circle, Bandywood Road, and Lambeth Road to Collingwood Drive.		90 number abandoned on southern routes.
	2/87	*Extended as* S3 service from Baldwins Lane to Shirley Station.		90 number abandoned on northern routes.
91	28/2/1971	Southbound to Baldwins Lane		
	1/6/1975		Converted to OMO	
92	28/2/1971	Pheasey, Kingstanding, Perry Barr, Lozells to Hockley and City, (Carrs Lane), then via Sparkbrook and Sparkhill to Stratford Road, Hall Green, (City Boundary).		From City to Hall Green replaced 37 route.
	6/4/1975	City, (Carrs Lane), via Stratford Road to Hall Green, (City Boundary) *extended* via Shirley to Cranmore Boulevard, Monkspath.		
	3/8/1975		Converted to OMO	
	c.1981	*Extended to* Widney Lane, Monkspath Hall Road.		
5	26/10/1986	**Replaced 91 service** City, (Carrs Lane), Sparkbrook, Sparkhill, Springfield, Sarehole Mill, Baldwins Lane, Shirley, Monkspath & Widney Manor to Solihull Station.		Cross-City connection abandoned.
6	26/10/1986	**Replaced 92 service**, City, (Carrs Lane), to Shirley via Blossomfield Road / Marshall Lake to Solihull Station.		Cross-City connection abandoned.

End Piece

From a major cross-city route, developed some eighty-five years ago in 1928 as the 29 route serving the north and south sides of Birmingham, a complex series of routes was developed as the need arose. This eventually resulted in passengers being able to travel from either Pheasey Estate in Aldridge (29A), Kingstanding Circle (29) or from the heart of the huge Kingstanding municipal housing area at Finchley Road (25, 33, 34) into the city via Lozells and Hockley, with its rich mixture of late Victorian villas, heavy industry and precious metal and jewellery manufacture. A further cross-city service (34) was added to the 33 route and ploughed an increasingly redundant furrow during peak periods to the extreme western side of the city at Quinton via Five Ways, Hagley Road and Hagley Road West. Various streets were traversed within the city centre but after the mid-1930s the One-Way Street scheme enabled services to use the city centre 'loop', unaltered for over fifty years. Originally the 29 route left the central area by way of a somewhat circuitous route through the wholesale markets area; after November 1934 the service settled down to travel from the early Victorian suburb of Camp Hill, through Sparkbrook and Sparkhill before reaching the Edwardian shopping area at Springfield. The original 29 route then went further along Stratford Road to Fox Hollies Road before turning right into Highfield Road and terminating within sight of Yardley Wood Station. The 29A, the second-longest bus route in Birmingham, left Stratford Road and, after reaching the sylvan delights of Wake Green Road, Colebank Road and the adjacent Sarehole Mill, went for a ramble around the 1930s suburbia of Hall Green to terminate at Baldwins Lane.

The passage of time has not been kind to the cross-city elements of the old 29, 29A and 33/34 services, as they do not exist anymore! Yet with one change of bus the old 29A route can still be ridden from its original 1936 terminus as a 33 from Pheasey Estate to Dale End in the centre of Birmingham, then a short walk to Moor Street station and on to Baldwins Lane and beyond on the 5 bus route. Not bad for a seventy-four-year-old bus service!

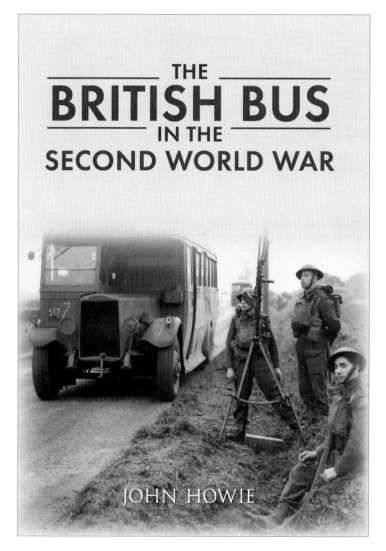

The British Bus in the Second World War

John Howie

The story of how British bus manufacturers and operators survived
the Second World War.

978 1 4456 1708 4
160 pages

Available from all good bookshops or order direct
from our website www.amberleybooks.com

Highland Buses
John Sinclair

This fascinating selection of photographs shows Highland
Omnibuses at its peak in the 1960s and 1970s, as well as the
isolated communities the company served and the stunning
landscapes in which it operated.

978 1 4456 1473 1
96 pages, full colour

Available from all good bookshops or order direct
from our website www.amberleybooks.com